RECOGNITION AT WORK

Acknowledgments

Editor/Project Leader
Dan Cafaro

Contributing Editors
Andrea Ozias
Barbara Parus
Bonnie Serino

Technical Reviewers
Daniel V. Lezotte, Ph.D.
Organizational Strategies Inc.

Karin Hollohan, CCP
Colorado Springs Utilities

Research
Betty Laurie
Wendy McMorine

Design
Alan Luu
Kris Sotelo

Production Manager
Rebecca Williams Ficker

WorldatWork.®
The Professional Association for
Compensation, Benefits and Total Rewards

WorldatWork is the world's leading not-for-profit professional association dedicated to knowledge leadership in compensation, benefits and total rewards. Founded in 1955, WorldatWork focuses on human resources disciplines associated with attracting, retaining and motivating employees. Besides serving as the membership association of the professions, the WorldatWork family of organizations provides education, certification (Certified Compensation Professional – CCP®, Certified Benefits Professional® – CBP and Global Remuneration Professional – GRP®), publications, knowledge resources, surveys, conferences, research and networking. WorldatWork Society of Certified Professionals; Alliance for Work-Life Progress (AWLP); and ITAC, The Telework Advisory Group are part of the WorldatWork family.

WorldatWork
14040 N. Northsight Blvd., Scottsdale, AZ 85260
480/951-9191   Fax 480/483-8352
www.worldatwork.org

Table of Contents

INTRODUCTION

Why Should Organizations Offer Recognition Programs?

As organizations continue to vie for a shrinking workforce, recognition becomes an important part of the total work experience. While recognition continues to be a missing link, few organizations have made it an important aspect of work life. Recognition is more than the occasional "thank you" or pat on the back. It involves a total commitment by the organization and its leadership. To begin, it is important to differentiate between reward and recognition.

Recognition involves identifying and reinforcing positive work performance. Its basic premise is that employees want to be acknowledged and valued for their contributions to the organization. Rewards involve giving something of value to recognize positive work results. Rewards are an integral part of any recognition program. This book will help organizations develop a recognition program that will make a positive impact on the employee's work experience.

Fred Herzberg, in his classic study of "satisfiers" versus "dissatisfiers" in the workplace, identified recognition as a satisfier or motivational factor. According to Herzberg, salary, supervision, working conditions and other work factors will at best prevent employees from being dissatisfied with their work environment. Herzberg identified recognition as "that which is received by an individual from any source with the accomplishment or achievement of a task or job." Further, it "involves noticing, praising and even blaming employees." However, the most compelling reason for offering a recognition program is the impact it has on companies that do. *Fortune's* annual list of "100 Best Companies to Work For" is a living testimony for recognition programs. Figure 1 (next page) provides some examples of unique programs provided by America's top companies. All are focused on recruiting, retaining and valuing employees. These programs are innovative, enlightening and in some cases provocative. Yet, there is no denying the end results. Recognition has been instrumental in reducing turnover, increasing productivity and in general creating a positive working environment.

Recognition is an important component of the organization's total rewards program. A good total rewards program includes compensation, benefits and the "work experience." The work experience component of total rewards includes recognition and programs geared toward work-life needs. A 2000 Hewitt Associates study that examined 1,020 U.S. employers offers staggering results. The study shows that work-life programs have increased tremendously from 1994 to 1999. Companies should seek innovative ways to recognize

FIGURE 1: EMPLOYEE RECOGNITION PROGRAMS		
Type	**Description**	**Examples**
Cash awards	Programs that provide either a fixed cash award or are based on a percent of the employee's pay. Some cash awards programs can provide additional employee benefits that have a stipulated dollar value. Note: Some programs are noted in parentheses.	• Lump-sum bonus • Cash incentive • Additional paid time off (employee benefit program) • Stock options • Paid trips • Stock award programs • Gift certificates • Specialized training (can be tied to the tuition program) • Prize program tied to earning points • Concierge services (employee benefit program that can be offered to recognize employees over a specific time period)
Spot programs	Recognition programs that have low or minimal cost and do not require a formal plan document or extensive administration.	• Movie tickets • Small-dollar value items (company merchandise, T-shirts, pens, key chains, etc.) • Paid meals • Balloons • Flowers • Tickets to special events
Symbolic awards	Recognition programs designed to provide a tangible award or memento.	• Service awards • Quality awards • Recognition certificates • Plaques and trophies
Verbal recognition	This approach provides praise directly to the individual or team.	• Thank-you card • Testimonies from senior leadership • Customer feedback • Written congratulations placed in the employee's record • Public recognition

achievement and address those critical work-life needs. Even though these programs appear to be the biggest growth area in the total rewards program, some employers still resist addressing the critical need for recognition.

Common Excuses for Resisting Recognition Programs

Individuals who see recognition as a "program of the month" challenge using it as a long-term business strategy. According to these recognition assassins, recognition programs only have temporary value to the employee and organization. These individuals refuse to believe that these programs are becoming important to the modern organization. Figure 2 (next page) lists some of the "common excuses" for not giving recognition to employees and how to overcome them. Later in this publication, more detail will be given on how to overcome the resistance to incorporating recognition into the corporate landscape.

This book establishes a framework that can be used to overcome the common excuses identified in Figure 2. It will address the financial and management aspects of developing an effective recognition program. The following six objectives are the foundation for this book. They are suggested to eliminate the need for excuses in not providing recognition programs. Each objective is incorporated into a comprehensive guide to designing and implementing these programs. Each objective also is mindful of the driving need to offer a program that will meet the organization's changing needs.

Objectives

1. To provide a method for assessing the organization's readiness to implement a recognition program
2. To offer a detailed approach for developing a recognition program
3. To review legal and tax requirements for providing a program
4. To develop implementation strategies and ongoing management guidelines
5. To provide methods for evaluating program effectiveness
6. To identify ongoing resources and program references.

Business Drivers

There are many reasons to offer employee recognition programs. But equally important to consider are the major business drivers. Recognition does the following:

- Is a valuable tool for recruiting and retaining qualified employees
- Serves as a catalyst for improving customer service by reinforcing positive employee performance
- Rewards positive contributions to product and service quality
- Provides a method for recognizing improvements in productivity
- Positively impacts morale and loyalty to the organization

FIGURE 2: COMMON EXCUSES FOR NOT GIVING EMPLOYEE RECOGNITION	
Excuse	**How to Address the Excuse**
"It's too expensive to offer."	• Most recognition programs are less than 10 percent of the overall total rewards program. • The cost of providing recognition is more than offset by reduction in recruitment and training costs. • The direct impact that recognition has on quality, customer service, employee morale and employee productivity actually makes it profitable to provide these programs.
"It has no long-term value to the employee."	• Recognition programs build loyalty and commitment. • Recognition establishes the organization as a unique, caring employer.
"Recognition leads to built-in expectations."	• Recognition should reinforce positive results and build organizational commitment. • Program expectations should be clearly communicated to all stakeholders.
"It becomes a never-ending process."	• Recognition should be meaningful and easily understood. • For recognition to be meaningful, it must be an ongoing process and not a temporary approach. • It must be internalized by leadership and become an accepted approach for managing employees.
"It creates competition among employees."	• If communicated properly to all key stakeholders, it fosters a sense of organizational pride and a spirit of individual and team accomplishment.
"No one recognizes me." (Note: This is an excuse given by supervisors who are rarely recognized.)	• A good recognition program makes it possible to include all employees in the process. • There should be a variety of approaches that will allow all employees to feel part of the program.
"I feel uncomfortable giving or receiving recognition."	• Leaders should be trained to give recognition. • Employees should be provided appropriate information about the program to fully understand the value of the recognition. • Employee input must be solicited to build a program that is supported and meets the needs of those being recognized.
"The employee is already being paid for doing his or her job."	• Recognition is an integral part of the total rewards program.

FIGURE 2: COMMON EXCUSES FOR NOT GIVING EMPLOYEE RECOGNITION (CONTINUED)	
"Recognition should be reserved for the performance evaluation."	• Recognition is time sensitive and should be provided as close as possible to the positive work performance. • Recognition is not an afterthought, but should be used as a management tool. • Continuous recognition of performance reinforces good work habits and sets a target for employees to achieve.
"Recognition creates confusion on what should be recognized."	• A good recognition program has detailed guidelines for what is to be recognized. • The purpose and methods to be used must be communicated to all key stakeholders. • Program expectations should be widely communicated and understood by all key stakeholders.

- Enhances the financial outlook of the organization by keeping employee costs down and increasing profit potential by providing better products and services.

When employees realize that their contributions are important to the organization's success, they are more likely to see themselves as partners and embrace the organization's goals, mission and values.

For recognition to become a vital part of the organization, it needs to be supported by leadership and internalized by all key stakeholders. When recognition has organizational support, the possibilities for success are unlimited.

1

Assessing the Current Organization's Readiness

Before implementing a recognition program, it is imperative that the organization assesses its readiness. It also is important to determine the impact on key stakeholders as part of the overall assessment. Who are these key stakeholders? They are individuals who need to be knowledgeable about and supportive of the program's success. The following checklist provides questions that should identify the key stakeholders in the recognition process:

Checklist for Identifying Key Stakeholders

1. Does this individual materially impact the program's success?

        ____YES   ____NO

2. Is this individual directly involved in managing the program's operations for his or her unit, department or division?

        ____YES   ____NO

3. Will this individual need to receive training if a new program is adopted?

        ____YES   ____NO

4. Has this individual expressed a desire to be involved in the design and implementation of the process?

        ____YES   ____NO

5. Will this individual be directly or indirectly involved in marketing the program?

        ____YES   ____NO

6. Does this individual directly or indirectly impact the program's financial success?

        ___YES   ____NO

7. Will this individual be actively involved in rolling out the new program?

        ___YES   ____NO

8. Is this individual a major decision-maker in reviewing and approving the program?

        ____YES   ____NO

9. Will this individual directly or indirectly benefit from the program?

        ____YES   ____NO

10. Will this individual be directly involved in the program's ongoing review and administration?

    ____YES   ____NO

A "yes" response to any of the questions indicates that the individual is a key stakeholder to the program's success. Typical key stakeholders include the following:

- Employees
- Managers
- Executives
- Board members
- Human resources professionals
- Customers
- Vendors.

This list, of course, is only a beginning and may or may not be common to your organization.

Once the key stakeholders have been identified, the next step is to assess their knowledge and support level of the program. Figure 3 (Page 4) assesses these factors. This is a subjective rating that could change as the stakeholder is provided more knowledge about the program. Figure 3 has a space for completing action steps for increasing the knowledge or support of the key stakeholder.

The simple assessment provided in Figure 3 is a starting point for identifying training and communications needs for key stakeholders.

FIGURE 3: ASSESSING KEY STAKEHOLDERS			
Key Question: Who Are the Key Stakeholders Who Need to be Knowledgeable and Supportive for Success?			
	Current Level of Knowledge	Current Level of Support	
Key Stakeholder	Low 1 2 3 4 5 High	Low 1 2 3 4 5 High	Action Step
Example Employee	1	3	Conduct Employee Meetings Survey Employees Conduct Focus Groups
Managers	2	4	Solicit Input on Plan Design Conduct Training Do Role Plays

Completing the Readiness Process

The organization must fully be ready to embrace recognition as an integral part of its operations. The following checklist provides a basic "readiness assessment" that can be used to determine if the organization is willing to accept and implement a recognition program.

Readiness Checklist

1 Does the organization have a commitment from top management to provide an employee recognition program?

     ___YES   ___NO

2. Is the organization committed to soliciting input from employees, managers, customers and other key stakeholders regarding the design and implementation of the program?

     ___YES   ___NO

3. Is the organization willing to commit financial support and resources to the program?

     ___YES   ___NO

4. Has the organization identified who will take the lead in designing, communicating and implementing the program?

    ___YES   ___NO

5. Is there a commitment to train managers and supervisors about the program?

    ___YES   ___NO

6. Is the organization willing to fully communicate the program and its importance to employees?

    ___YES   ___NO

7. Are managers and supervisors supportive of making recognition a priority in how they lead and manage employees?

    ___YES   ___NO

8. Do employees view recognition as important to their work experience?

    ___YES   ___NO

9. Is the organization willing and able to provide a new program at this point in its operations?

    ___YES   ___NO

10. Does the organization have the ability to monitor the program's effectiveness and its impact on the organization?

    ___YES   ___NO

Note: Total the "yes" and "no" responses. If there are eight or more "yes" responses, the organization is ready to consider an employee recognition program.

Determining Support from Above

Some organizations view recognition as a high-risk venture that adds very little to productivity and the bottom line. The readiness assessment is a valuable tool in determining risk tolerance. Three questions can be added to the readiness assessment to determine what level of financial commitment and risk the organization is willing to support.

Answer the questions below using the following rating scale:

1 = No support financially or organizationally

2 = Minimal financial support and supervisory effort should
   be provided

3 = Moderate budgetary and organizational commitment should
   be made

4 = Organization should make a strong financial commitment to
   the program

5 = Program should have top priority in its development and
   implementation

1. At what level should the organization fund employee recognition?

   1   2   3   4   5

2. At what level should recognition programs be funded, compared to other total rewards programs such as base compensation and employee benefits?

   1   2   3   4   5

3. At what level should the organization commit financial, supervisory and other resources to the implementation and development of an employee recognition program?

   1   2   3   4   5

Senior leadership should complete the readiness assessment first to determine the risk tolerance they are willing to support. Department directors should answer these same questions to determine their support and their willingness to make recognition an integral part of their departmental budget. Depending on financial limitations and other program implementations, these questions can be used to establish a financial commitment based on a percentage of the total rewards budget.

The composition of the senior leadership group should include the chief executive officer, chief operating officer or most senior operational vice president, chief financial officer and the senior human resources leader. This group can be expanded to include other key formal and informal leaders. At some point, it is important to ask for input from informal leaders. These individuals know the organization's pulse and will help sell the program's importance to employees.

The readiness process helps determine how committed an organization is to providing financial, human and time-based resources. Time-based resources involves allowing employees and managers appropriate time to learn and internalize the program. If managers and employees are not given adequate time to fully understand the program's importance, it will never be successful. The time-based resource also refers to the organization's ability to accept and embrace a new program at this point in time. If the organization is in the midst of a number of key projects and changes, it may not be the best time to offer another program. It may cause communication overload and result in the tuning out of the program by key stakeholders.

While the assessment provides a glimpse into the cultural impact of implementing a new program, it is important to ensure there are no political or cultural obstacles. A simple questionnaire can be used to conduct a cultural audit to determine if the climate is ripe for a recognition program. Figure 4 (Page 8) provides a sample questionnaire that should be administered to a representative sample of employees, supervisors, informal leaders, senior management and other key stakeholders.

The responses to the questions in Figure 4 can be an eye-opener for some organizations. If possible, the organization should sample at least 25 to 50 key stakeholders to determine if there are any statistically valid trends uncovered during the audit process. Some organizations go one step further and use the questionnaire as a mini-survey or payroll stuffer. The problem with using a widespread approach is that built-in expectations are often created with employees and other key stakeholders. If the organization decides not to implement a recognition program, it can be devastating if it has solicited employee feedback.

The readiness process should reveal if there are political problems, organizational support, training needs and overall program interest. However, the readiness assessment or cultural audit does not address the program's financial impact, both in terms of cost and impact on productivity and revenue.

Addressing the Various Impacts

There are a number of key factors in addressing the financial, human and organizational impact of a recognition program. They include the following:

FIGURE 4: SAMPLE CULTURAL AUDIT

Instructions: For each of the following statements, circle a number to indicate your estimation of the organization's present state or skill level to provide an employee recognition program.

Scale: 1 = Strongly Disagree
       2 = Disagree
       3 = Neutral (Neither Agree Nor Disagree)
       4 = Agree
       5 = Strongly Agree

1. There are few organizational barriers in offering an employee recognition program.

        1 2 3 4 5

2. Managers have a good understanding of how to effectively recognize employees.

        1 2 3 4 5

3. The organization has a history of providing appropriate communication about new programs and other major changes.

        1 2 3 4 5

4. The organization has a history of accepting change and acting on it in a positive manner.

        1 2 3 4 5

5. Employees have a relatively high understanding of recognition programs and the work behaviors that should be rewarded.

        1 2 3 4 5

6. There is a commitment to provide time to train employees and managers about the recognition program.

        1 2 3 4 5

7. Our employees and managers would view implementing a recognition program as a challenge, rather than a threat.

        1 2 3 4 5

8. This program will be fully supported by the senior leadership of the organization.

        1 2 3 4 5

9. There are no potential barriers to providing a recognition program.

    1 2 3 4 5

10. There is little or no need for a recognition program in the organization.

    1 2 3 4 5

Please make any comments about the organization's ability to make recognition an important part of its culture:

_____
_____
_____
_____
_____

- **Organization Size** — Generally a larger organization will need to invest more dollars into recognition because of the number of employees. However, some smaller organizations are more committed to rewarding and recognizing their employees. Size only becomes a financial consideration if the organization is committed and willing to invest in recognition.
- **Training** — The time and expense for training supervisors and employees represent a significant amount of the overall program cost. If the organization takes shortcuts to training, the program's effectiveness and support will be compromised.
- **Administrative Support** — One individual should be designated by the organization to coordinate the program. This individual is responsible for overseeing training, ongoing administration and initial program implementation. Other administrative support could include a full-time secretary or other clerical position, a part-time trainer, an individual who can provide technological and computer expertise and a general assistant if the program becomes too large for one individual to handle.
- **Equipment** — The biggest equipment needs include computers, audio-visual equipment, kiosks for checking program updates, office furniture, training room furniture and ancillary computer companion equipment such as printers, scanners and monitors.
- **Supplies** — The biggest need would be the cost of printing brochures

and providing copies of policies to key stakeholders. Other ongoing needs would be the usual office supplies such as paper, pens, pencils, folders and postage.

- **Marketing** — Marketing involves all the costs associated with sparking enthusiasm and providing basic program information. It generally includes time needed to create brochures, information releases to employees and the overall program communications plan. Some cost can be shared with the in-house marketing department. Consultants and other creative marketing approaches can be purchased from outside sources.

- **Software** — Software packages used off the shelf or customized to the organization are invaluable in training participants and tracking program success.

- **Types of Rewards Offered** — The type of recognition program will determine the size of the reward provided. A formal program tied to measurable goals and incentives will generally cost more to offer than spot recognition. The organization needs to decide early on how extensive it wants the program to be. Generally, it is best to cap formal programs at a reasonable level during the first year of operation to determine if the investment has been worthwhile in terms of impact on performance and productivity. This also holds true for spot recognition, which should be used prudently and not as a program to give away "free stuff."

Figure 5 (Page 12) provides sample budget items utilizing some of the key financial areas previously discussed. The column on "Cost/Revenue Offsets" provides suggestions on how to best utilize the key financial areas. Dollar amounts have been omitted because of the ever-changing cost of labor, supplies and equipment.

A recognition program's total cost can range from $70,000 to several million dollars depending on the program's scope and objectives. Because it can be a substantial investment, it is important to monitor the impact that the program can have on critical factors such as revenue, employee retention and productivity. In the three circle diagrams (See Figure 6, Page 14), each organization realized a gain by offering a recognition program. Organization A is a smaller company that was able to tie the impact of recognition to net revenue. Organization A focused on how recognition affected customer service, employee performance and quality improvement. All three of those areas then had a direct or indirect effect on net revenue.

Organization B was most concerned with employee retention. It was determined by Organization B that it cost approximately $20,000 to replace and train a new employee. The recognition program in this case was responsible for retaining 44 full-time equivalent employees (i.e., $880,000) based on historical turnover and employee feedback.

Organization C honed in on the relationship between recognition and productivity. Based on a before and after comparison, the formal recognition program implemented by Organization C increased productivity by 10 percent, which resulted in a $504,000 net gain. The analysis of how recognition impacts the business, of course, can be very detailed. However, the organization can get a good idea of how the program is doing by conducting a four-step review:

Step One — Link the program with organizational goals and needs. Chapter 2 will address goals and objectives in more detail. The circle diagrams looked at three areas that have identifiable financial results (i.e., generated revenue, turnover cost and productivity). The bottom line is to link the financial impact with what is truly important to the organization.

Step Two — Compare final plan costs to what was budgeted for recognition. As with other total rewards programs, the cost for administering a recognition program should be monitored and justified.

Step Three — Review the plan's financial impact with the executive team. This gives the executive firsthand knowledge of how the program is performing from a financial perspective. The financial impact generally leaves a more lasting impression with executives than simply giving a summary of how many employees were recognized during the previous quarter.

Step Four — Use the review process to determine if the program should be revised, eliminated or continued in its present form. The analysis should provide data that indicate if employee recognition is worthwhile financially. To compare the program's impact, a number of valuable benchmark resources can be used.

	FIGURE 5: SAMPLE BUDGET ITEMS	
Key Financial Area(s)	**Cost/Revenue Offsets**
ADMINISTRATIVE SUPPORT	
Program coordinator	This position can double as a benefits analyst if the program is small. The director of compensation and benefits or employee relations director can assist with program design and oversee the overall process.
Program assistant	Depending on the size of the program, this position may not be needed. If it is needed, this position may be able to take on additional duties and projects.
Clerical support	This position could be used to do other duties and jobs depending on program demands. However, even a small program will need some clerical support.
Trainer/educator	The program coordinator can perform the training function. Even in larger programs, this position may only need to be part time.
EQUIPMENT	
Computers	Computers can be used for other organizational programs or processes depending on the size the program.
Printers, monitors, scanners	Again, this equipment and other technology needs can be put to others uses.
Audio-Visual Equipment	The investment amount will be determined by the size of the organization and the training needs. This equipment can be used by many different programs.
Office furniture	This may not be needed if existing space is utilized.
Training	Remodeling existing space or training participants in small-group settings could save money. Note: It is important to invest in training if the program is to be fully communicated.
SOFTWARE	If the software is customized for the recognition program, it will probably not have any alternative uses. Some customized software can be part of a larger monitoring and statistical package, which has many uses.

FIGURE 5: SAMPLE BUDGET ITEMS (CONTINUED)	
SUPPLIES	
Office supplies	All of these supplies could be used for other programs and processes.
Program brochures	Program brochures can be used in conjunction with recruitment information as a selling point to join the organization.
MARKETING	
Creative design	Costs will depend on whether or not internal resources are used. Using the organization's marketing and human resources department to help design marketing materials can avoid high consultant costs. Note: This expense item only includes marketing costs and not program design.
Printing costs	This expense is different then the cost of program brochures. It includes initial creative design, special printing needs and a supply of printed materials to be distributed to participants and key stakeholders.
PROGRAM COST	
Program	Consultants are paid handsomely to design recognition programs. Any time spent by the organization in program design will save money.
Formal recognition program	The organization will need to establish dollar limits before implementation. Even small organizations will need to invest a minimum of $10,000 for the recognition to have any impact. An offset would be to tie the program to measurable outcomes such as customer satisfaction.
Informal or spot recognition programs	The big offset for this type of program is the direct impact on morale. A minimum investment of $5,000 is recommended because it indicates commitment by the organization. Most large organizations may want to cap this program at $100,000 for the first year of operation.

Benchmarking Against Best Practices

The parameters to benchmark against must be established before seeking comparative data. Figure 7 (Page 16) details some common parameters that can be used. The checklist can assist the organization in determining what to benchmark. This data is useful in designing successful recognition programs. Benchmarking also can assist the organization in assessing its current effectiveness in employee recognition. The most important benchmark tool comes from within the organization. What does the organization want to achieve by offering a recognition program? This can be determined by ranking problem

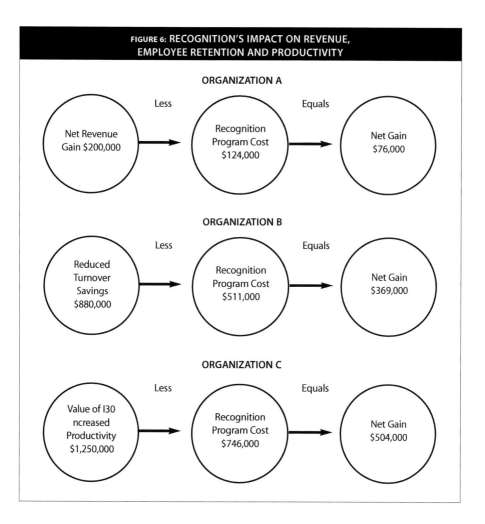

FIGURE 6: RECOGNITION'S IMPACT ON REVENUE, EMPLOYEE RETENTION AND PRODUCTIVITY

ORGANIZATION A

Net Revenue Gain $200,000 — Less → Recognition Program Cost $124,000 — Equals → Net Gain $76,000

ORGANIZATION B

Reduced Turnover Savings $880,000 — Less → Recognition Program Cost $511,000 — Equals → Net Gain $369,000

ORGANIZATION C

Value of I30 ncreased Productivity $1,250,000 — Less → Recognition Program Cost $746,000 — Equals → Net Gain $504,000

areas that recognition could possibly impact. For example, do we seek to improve customer satisfaction? We could build a recognition program that rewards employees who treat customers with respect and care.

The 10 factors used to determine *Fortune's* "100 Best Companies to Work For" list (See Figure 8, Page 17) give insight into what to incorporate in a recognition program. These same factors should be used to monitor, design, communicate and implement a recognition program. For example, The Container Store (ranked No. 1 by *Fortune* in 2001 and No. 2 in 2002) instills teamwork and family values, and recognizes individuals for contributing to the overall organizational success. The Container Store's turnover rate is 28 percent versus a 73.6 percent industry average. Microsoft, a perennial top company, custom designs its organization to accommodate the special talents of the individual. Finally, Medtronic has created a positive workplace by offering an environment that allows employee input and fosters individual growth.

This list is by no means exhaustive and should correspond to the organization's culture. The internal inventory is the last step in the assessment process. The organization is now ready to begin developing program objectives and integrating recognition into the total rewards program.

FIGURE 7: CHECKLIST OF BENCHMARK PARAMETERS

____ **Time Frame:** Do we want to compare annual, quarterly or, if available, monthly data?

____ **Revenue Size:** Is it important to seek data from organizations with comparable revenues? Note: In some cases it is more important to seek out companies with larger or smaller revenue sizes to have a frame of reference of what works well in organizations that have the financial ability to offer different levels of benefits.

____ **Product/Service:** Do we want to compare to organizations in the same line of business?

____ **Number of Employees:** Will we want data from organizations that have a comparable size workforce?

____ **Profitability:** What level of profitability, return on investment or other financial indicator do we want to compare against?

____ **Employee Turnover:** How does the industry turnover rate compare to our rate after implementing a recognition program? How does recognition impact employee turnover in other comparable organizations?

____ **Current Programs in Place:** Do we simply want to review how other organizations with current recognition programs are doing?

____ **Quality Outcomes:** How has employee recognition impacted quality in comparable organizations?

____ **Service Initiatives:** How has recognition affected service delivery and customer satisfaction in other organizations?

- Recruiting, hiring and orientation
- Development and learning
- Work environment
- Rewards and recognition
- Health and well-being
- Work/life programs
- Financial security
- Organizational structure
- Organizational culture
- "Unique" people practices.

Rewards and recognition were an essential part of 100 Best Companies inventory. The best companies realize that recognition is vital to their existence. Also, this inventory included "unique" people practices as one of its indicators. Some of the more unique people practices included:

- Flexible work schedules for high performers
- Family-oriented work environments
- Employee involvement teams
- Special employee celebrations
- Recognition bonuses
- Concierge services such as dry cleaning, take-out food, etc. for high performers
- Weekend retreats
- All-expenses-paid trips to exotic places such as Maui
- Point systems that allow employees to receive cash or prizes for unique contributions.

A closer look revealed that many of these "unique" people practices were really recognition approaches that reached out to the employee personally and individually. As the organization defines what is important to include in its own recognition program, an internal inventory can be developed to benchmark what is important to the organization's success. Some meaningful internal inventory indicators include the following:

- Organizational morale
- Job vacancy rates
- Turnover rate
- Internal transfers
- Promotions
- Customer satisfaction scores
- Cost per unit
- Work process improvements
- Production turn-around rates
- Turn-around time to fill a vacant position
- Changes/projects currently facing the organization.

2

Establishing Program Objectives

Figure 9 details the characteristics of an effective employee recognition program. All of these characteristics will be discussed in this publication. Let's focus on the first three in this section.

FIGURE 9: CHARACTERISTICS OF AN EFFECTIVE EMPLOYEE RECOGNITION PROGRAM	
Identify Responsible Parties	• One individual should be identified as the in-house coordinator. • Recognition should be established as a priority for all organizational leaders. • The chief executive officer (CEO) should identify who is responsible for program success.
Develop Goals And Objectives	• Establish 3 to 4 program goals or objectives. • Goals and objectives should reflect what the organization is trying to accomplish by implementing a program. • Goals should be succinct and easy to understand.
Establish Key Indicators Of Success	• Develop 2 or 3 key indicators of program success. • Tie key indicators to the program goals and objectives.
Develop Easily Understood Eligibility Criteria	• Criteria should be understood by participants and key stakeholders. • Avoid using complicated formulas to determine recognition. • Criteria should be few in number and not an exhaustive list of requirements.
Build In Cost Containment Features	• Establish reward levels and cap dollar limits. • The recognition budget should be predetermined and not a moving target. • Tie recognition cost to the financial success of the organization.
Communicate Program's Importance	• Provide complete and updated information about the program. • Survey participants and key stakeholders on a regular basis and ask for input about the program. • Provide ongoing communication about the program.

Establish Ownership Responsibility

It is imperative to name one individual to coordinate and nurture the recognition program. This individual is responsible for program development, oversight and goal setting. The person placed in this coordinator role should possess experience with tracking, designing and communicating a program of this magnitude. In addition, the individual should have familiarity with general operations and have a high profile of trust and respect throughout the organization. The person should be seen as approachable and committed to developing a program that meets the organizational needs. Figure 10 (Page 22) summarizes some key roles and responsibilities of the program coordinator. It should be noted this individual may or may not be part of the human resources department. This person needs to be seen as an objective resource who can bridge the needs of a diverse workforce.

The employee recognition team has the chief responsibility of assisting the program coordinator in developing and implementing the recognition program. This team consists of eight to 10 key individuals who have a direct interest in the program's success. The composition of the team depends on the design and needs of the organization. A typical team could include leaders and key executives from the following areas of responsibility (Note: Not all of the disciplines listed need to be permanent team members):

- Finance
- Human resources
- Marketing
- Operations
- General services
- Legal compliance (Note: This can be the organization's legal counsel or compliance officer)
- Payroll
- Administration.

It is important to have a recognition team that has individuals who are committed to recognition and want to serve as the program's chief architects and torchbearers. Before accepting assignment on the team, each individual should answer the following honestly:

1. Do I have enough time to commit to this program? Note: The initial time commitment would be 40 to 60 hours to plan and implement the program. Ongoing commitment is four to eight hours monthly to review program progress with the coordinator.
2. Am I really committed to implementing a recognition program?
3. Do I feel recognition is important for the organization to carry out now?
4. Am I prepared to support the program to top management and the board if necessary?
5. Will I be comfortable being a member of a highly visible and possibly controversial team?

Before serving on a recognition team, the individual must be able to respond "yes" to all five of the above questions. The team also can assist in developing training approaches that will address the specific needs of individual

FIGURE 10: ROLES AND RESPONSIBILITIES OF THE PROGRAM COORDINATOR	
Roles and Responsibilities	**Principal Accountabilities**
Program Design	• Assists in design of the program including developing eligibility criteria • Coordinates and administers readiness assessment with organizational leaders • Coordinates or conducts a survey of employees to determine design features.
Policy Formulation	• Develops and writes policies and procedures • Participates in developing specific program guidelines to ensure consistent program administration.
Communication	• Participates in designing a formal communication plan for the program • Assures ongoing communication is provided about the program and any modifications which are made.
Training	• Conducts initial training with key stakeholders about the program. • Coordinates ongoing training.
Program/Legal Compliance	• Ensures program is administered equitably and in accordance with approved guidelines • Reviews program concerns and complaints • Maintains an awareness of applicable laws and regulations that govern cash and noncash employee rewards programs.
Monitoring	• Develops statistical indicators to assess program success • Conducts periodic audit of indicators and reports results to the recognition team • Works with organizational leaders from each department or work unit to develop specific monitors • Conducts annual program audit to ensure program is being appropriately administered.
Ongoing Coordination	• Serves as the focal point for ongoing program development and continued maintenance of recognition activities • Functions as the major resource to the employee recognition program • Serves as the coordinating body for ongoing program development. • Oversees any program changes • Presents quarterly updates to the management team, and board of directors as appropriate, about program impact and utilization • Identifies potential areas of improvement • Identifies ongoing training and communication needs • Solicits feedback about the program from key stakeholders on at least an annual basis.

departments/units. This is especially important since each department/unit generally will have varying degrees of support and understanding of the program's impact. It will take a well-structured training effort to solidify the program's impact and worth to the individual. A recognition team, by virtue of its diversity and makeup, should be able to identify what will work best for a particular department or geographic location. Finally, the team functions as a creative cabinet to the program coordinator. Creativity will keep the program fresh and kindle enthusiasm from key stakeholders.

While the program coordinator and recognition team provide guidance and direction, the final responsibility for the program rests with those individuals who are performing and observing excellent work performance. Figure 11 (Page 24) addresses the all-important question regarding recognition: "Whose job is this?" It is not too surprising that the ultimate responsibility for a good recognition program permeates throughout the organization. Those responsible include executives, managers, employees, customers, guests, vendors and even the employee's family members.

The six statements addressed in Figure 11 are intended to emphasize the importance of including a wide range of key stakeholders in managing the program. Many times organizations forget the importance of the employee's family. The family often knows firsthand the contributions its loved one makes to the organization. As the program is implemented, the family should be kept informed about what it takes for the employee to be rewarded. The family then can lend its support to the program, generally making it more exciting and plausible for the employee.

Finally, recognition is the responsibility of everyone who comes in contact with the organization. The key stakeholders identified in Figure 11 are merely a few examples. Ultimately the company's CEO is responsible for any program's success. The CEO must fully support and extol the virtues of having employee recognition in place. If possible, the CEO either should select the program coordinator and/or the recognition team's members. The CEO should be kept informed and be involved in the program development and implementation. This involvement sends the message throughout the organization that everyone is responsible for the program's success.

FIGURE 11: WHOSE JOB IS THIS?		
Possible Key Statement	**Key Stake Holder**	**Response**
1. I believe recognition is important to the organization's success.	• Executives	Agree
	• Managers • Employees • Board members	Disagree
2. I personally have observed examples of excellent work performance that deserves some type of recognition.	• Executives	Agree
	• Managers • Employees • Customers • Guests • Vendors	Disagree
3. Some employees are reluctant to share specific work accomplishments with their supervisor.	• Co-workers	Agree
	• Managers • Employee family members (Note: Involving the family can give support and uniqueness)	Disagree
4. The organization has an excellent reputation for rewarding employees who do exceptional work.	• Employees	Agree
	• Managers • Community leaders • Customers	Disagree
5. There are programs already in place that encourage and reward high work performance.	• Employees	Agree
	• Managers	Disagree
6. Employee recognition is everyone's job.	• Executives	Agree
	• Managers • Employees • Customers	Disagree

Developing Goals and Objectives

An effective recognition program must have a solid foundation framed with distinct goals and objectives. The goals should be few and reflect what the organization is trying to achieve with the program. Figure 12 (Page 26) provides some sample objectives. These will be used to communicate the recognition efforts to key stakeholders. These objectives also will be instrumental in the basic program design as well as being an integral part of training key stakeholders. It is important that the recognition team, executive staff, human resources department and other key organizational leaders review these objectives.

The program objectives should be aligned with the organization's business strategy and mission. The four sample objectives in Figure 12 are built on four key business strategies:

- Improved Employee Performance and Productivity
- Excellent Customer Service
- Positive Employee Morale
- Increased Employee Retention.

Figure 12 also includes a "key stakeholder review list" for each objective. This list provides a final reminder of who should be reviewing and approving the final program objectives before they are communicated.

Some key stakeholders will be involved in all three levels of the approval/review process. It is important to keep key stakeholders on task when soliciting their input. The best way to do this is to be sure that the following questions are addressed before communicating goals and objectives:

1. What needs to be communicated?
2. Who is going to be affected by the program?
3. Why is it important for the key stakeholder to know about the goals and objectives?
4. When is the established deadline for completing the approval or review process?
5. How should the goals and objectives be communicated? Examples: training updates, personal memorandums, audio tape, e-mail, intranet, Internet, etc.

FIGURE 12: SAMPLE PROGRAM OBJECTIVES

Note: To make them effective tools, all four objectives are specific and measurable.
The "approval/review level" column for key stakeholders has three priority levels:
Level 1: Final Approval
Level 2: Feedback and Review
Level 3: Informational Only

Key Stakeholder Program Objectives	Approval/Review List	Review level
1. To provide a program to reward employees who exceed expected performance levels by at least 10 percent.	CEO	1
	Recognition Team	1,2
	Managers	2
	Program Coordinator	1,2
	Chief Financial Officer	1,2
	Employees	2,3
	Customers	3
	Board Members	1,2,3
	Vendors	3
2. To recognize employees who have made meaningful contributions to customer service as measured by survey data and personal feedback.	CEO	1
	Chief Marketing Executive	2,3
	Recognition Team	1,2
	Program Coordinator	1,2
	Managers	2,3
	Employees	2,3
	Customers	2,3
	Board Members	1,2,3
	Vendors	3
3. To create a more satisfying work environment for employees, which will be measured by achieving at least a 10 percent improvement in job satisfaction on the annual employee opinion survey.	CEO	1
	Chief HR Officer	2,3
	Recognition Team	1,2
	Program Coordinator	1,2
	Managers	2,3
	Employees	2,3
	Board Members	1,2,3
	Family Members	2,3
4. To provide a program that will align with other total rewards programs to reduce employee turnover by 20 percent.	CEO	1
	Chief HR Officer	1,2,3
	Recognition Team	1, 2
	Program Coordinator	1,2
	Recruitment and Retention Committee	2,3
	Managers	2,3
	Employees	2,3
	Board Members	1,2,3

The information obtained from these questions will allow the organization to move forward with the process. It also links goals and objectives with key program indicators.

Establishing Key Indicators

Establishing key indicators early in the development of the program provides an anchor for its goals and objectives. Key indicators are really an extension of these goals and objectives. They answer the burning question that all key stakeholders have about the program: How will we really know if it is successful? For this reason, there are a few key indicators to ensure that participants can grasp and fully understand what it takes to succeed. Most key indicators are built around at least two or three of the following strategic areas:

- Financial results
- Quality
- Service
- Performance/Productivity
- Job Satisfaction/Employee Morale
- Employee Retention.

It is important to remember that key indicators are not the only measures of program success. They focus on what is most important to the program's overall success. Figure 13 (Page 28) provides some sample key indicators built upon three of the strategic areas discussed. These indicators also can be linked back to strategic themes represented by the objectives provided in Figure 12. The key indicators will be vital in designing a recognition scorecard.

In this case, the CEO and employee recognition team have determined to emphasize the first three strategic areas in the first year of the program's operation. These are the most pressing issues for the organization at this time. The other strategic area will be measured as a stand-alone target and will be tied directly to the company's and individual employee's performance. For that reason, the performance/productivity measure often is linked to the employee's performance evaluation and is a more long-term recognition approach. Figure 14 (Page 24) is a potpourri of key indicators commonly used to measure the success of the six strategic areas. Obviously, this is not an all-inclusive list. The organization must decide what is important to focus on during the first year of the program's operation. Remember: Key indicators should be few and should reflect what is important to the company.

These indicators could be used to measure the success of other total rewards programs such as individual and organizationwide incentives. Focusing the indicators on how recognition has impacted each strategic area is what differentiates the application of the measures. For example, if employee morale is a strategic area of focus, recognition could be tracked to determine if it truly has had any impact on job satisfaction (e.g., opinion surveys, employee feedback and turnover). Again, selecting a few indicators and determining what is important to measure are key in determining the program's impact.

After the organization establishes what to incorporate in the program, key indicators then can be used to help monitor the program's impact on employees and the organization. Figure 14 illustrates that a solid recognition program has various ways to influence the company's success. The organization should

FIGURE 13: KEY INDICATORS			
Strategic Area	**Program Objective**	**Key Indicator**	**Target**
Service	Excellent customer service	Customer satisfaction scores	The organization will be at the 90th percentile or higher when compared to other similar organizations.
Employee Morale	Positive employee morale	Job satisfaction scores on the employee opinion survey	The organization is to improve overall job satisfaction score by at least 10%.
Employee Retention	Increased employee retention	Turnover and job vacancy rates	Reduce employee turnover by 20% and maintain a job vacancy rate of less than 10%.
Performance/ Productivity	Improved employee performance and productivity	Organizational and employee performance	Improve organizational productivity by at least 5% and or employee performance by 10%.

commit to making recognition an integral part of its total rewards program. Once this commitment is made, recognition becomes an essential tool for motivating and managing employees.

FIGURE 14: SAMPLE KEY INDICATORS BY STRATEGIC AREA		
Strategic Area	**Sample Key Indicator**	**Suggested Target/Measure**
Financial Results	• Return on investment • Cost per unit • Net revenue • Gross revenue • Bad debt expense • Nonsalary cost	• At least 5% • Cost savings as determined by program goals • A positive increase of at least 5% to 10 % • Increase of 10% of revenue • A positive reduction as determined by program goals • A positive reduction to be determined
Quality	• Product defects • Quality improvements • Key quality indicators • Quality controls	• A positive reduction in product returns • Documented improvements in work processes • Assessment of key quality indicators should exceed established standards • Quality audits are conducted on a regular basis to determine if product or service meets or exceeds established control limits
Service	• Customer satisfaction level • Wait times • Internal service approval rate • Service standard • Customer compliments	• Generally should be at the 90th percentile level if benchmark data is available. If not available, there should be a specific target for improving customer satisfaction based on survey data (e.g., 5% increase). • A reduction in the time it takes the customer to receive service or pay for the product • Surveying internal customers and recognizing employees for positive approval rates • The organization exceeds established service standards • Recognition or rewards tied to compliments directly received from customers
Performance/ Productivity	• Employee performance level(s) • Downtime • Output or service units • New product or service development	• Employee performance exceeds established rates (e.g., 10% improvement) • Reduced or eliminated production/service downtime or delays • Increased production or number of units sold or delivered • Individual or team input into new product or service development

FIGURE 14: SAMPLE KEY INDICATORS BY STRATEGIC AREA (CONTINUED)		
Job Satisfaction Employee Morale	• Job satisfaction rate • Employee grievances • Morale index	• Improved job satisfaction by 10% based on employee feedback • Number of grievances filed and resolved • Ongoing monitoring of morale on a divisional, department and unit level
Employee Retention	• Turnover rate • Job vacancy rate • Transfer process • Turnaround time to fill a vacant position	• Ensuring a percentage reduction in employee turnover • Reducing job vacancy rate will impact the morale and retention of current employees • Promoting internal employees to job opportunities • Meeting or exceeding the targets established for filling a job opening (e.g., from 21 days to 14 days)

3

Integrating Recognition into the Total Rewards Program

Four essential factors should be considered when aligning recognition with the organization's business strategy.

Factor 1

Involve senior leadership in program design. In fact, the program coordinator and recognition team should provide a first draft of the program to senior leadership for its input and review. By involving senior leadership, it prevents the program from becoming branded as "another feel-good program developed by the human resources department." Senior leadership should be involved with five key areas:

1. Program goals and objectives: As discussed in Chapter 2, senior leadership must be supportive of the program's goals and objectives. The goals and objectives should reflect the strategic themes that link the organization to the program.
2. Key indicators: Senior leaders should be able to articulate what is important to monitor to determine the program's success.
3. Incentives/Rewards: Senior leadership will need to approve the types and amounts of monetary incentives and rewards. A budget also will need to be developed for the program. Senior leadership will need to review and approve the program budget.
4. Program eligibility: Senior leadership should help determine program eligibility criteria. This includes identifying what behavior and performance will be recognized. It also includes who can do the recognition (e.g., managers, supervisors, peers, customers, etc.).
5. Program boundaries: Senior leadership should have input in establishing program boundaries. This includes establishing financial limits, program responsibility, and time commitments to training employees and managers about the program.

Factor 2

Incorporate funding requirements into the total rewards budget. In Chapter 1, the financial impact of developing a program was identified. Depending on the organization's size, program cost can range up to several million dollars. The bottom line is that most recognition efforts represent a major investment to the organization. This must be a planned investment and not happen as the program unfolds. Most organizations provide inadequate funds when implementing their recognition efforts. This is a big mistake. The funding for a rewards and recognition program should be incorporated into the total rewards budget. Just like compensation and benefits programs, recognition represents a vital part of the employee's overall rewards structure. Figure 15 (Page 34) provides a sample total rewards budget. The cost of providing a recognition program in Figure 15 is 1 percent of total base compensation (Note: This does not include the cost for annual bonuses that may or may not be performance-based).

Some organizations will choose to fund at a higher or lower level than the sample total rewards budget in Figure 15, but a recommended funding level would be 1 percent to 7 percent of base compensation.

In the sample total rewards budget in Figure 15, recognition programs were underestimated by $138,000. Unless monetary boundaries are carefully established, it is common for organizations to project costs below what is needed for the first year of operation. The first year is often exciting for managers and employees. Recognition is a tool that can be used easily, and rewards often are readily available to participants. For this reason, organizations should carefully assess their financial commitment and risk tolerance. If recognition is to become a valuable motivational tool, it must be appropriately funded. Lack of funding can shut down a program in midyear, which will leave participants wondering why the organization bothered implementing it in the first place.

Factor 3

Integrate recognition with the organization's mission, values and operating philosophy. The program's purpose should be built around the organization's mission and basic values. Consider the fictitious organization (i.e., Major Corporation) in the example and how it incorporates these important aspects. Notice how the recognition program closely resembles all these important organizational aspects. For example, the recognition program must be "value driven," which means it must match the organization's culture. Some additional values not addressed in the recognition link include the following:

- Innovation — promoting the creation of new ideas and changes
- Quality Improvement — encouraging process improvement
- Exceptional Performance — rewarding individuals who make outstanding contributions

FIGURE 15: TOTAL REWARDS BUDGET			
Type of Total Rewards Program	Budget	Actual	Variance
COMPENSATION			
Fixed Compensation	$35,000,000	$34,942,000	($58,000)
Annual Bonuses	1,750,000	1,775,000	+25,000
Shift Differential	2,100,000	2,100,000	0
Merit Salary Increases	1,400,000	1,450,000	+50,000
Market Salary Adjustments	2,000,000	1,950,000	(50,000)
Total Compensation Cost	**$42,250,000**	**$42,217,000**	**($33,000)**
BENEFITS PROGRAMS			
Mandatory Programs			
• FICA	$3,232,125	$3,229,600	($2,525)
• Workers' Compensation	565,000	565,000	0
• Unemployment Compensation	200,000	190,000	(10,000)
• Voluntary Programs			
- Medical Insurance	3,500,000	3,475,000	(25,000)
- Dental	465,000	475,000	+10,000
- Vision	100,000	100,000	0
- Retirement (401k)	2,300,000	2,320,000	+20,000
- Disability	350,000	336,000	(14,000)
- Prescription Drugs	300,000	290,000	(10,000)
- Disability	475,000	475,000	0
Total Benefits Cost	**$11,487,125**	**$11,455,600**	**($31,525)**
WORK EXPERIENCE PROGRAMS			
Recognition Programs			
• Cash Rewards	$320,000	$408,000	+$88,000
• Noncash Programs	30,000	77,000	+47,000
Work-Life Programs			
• Employee Assistance Program	65,000	71,000	+6,000
• Child Care	120,000	115,000	(5,000)
• Legal Assistance	60,000	60,000	0
Employee Fitness	50,000	52,000	+2,000
Financial Planning	15,000	15,000	0
Total "Work Experience" Cost	**$660,000**	**$798,000**	**+$138,000**
TOTAL COST OF TR PROGRAM	**$54,397,125**	**$54,470,600**	**+$73,475**

- Respect for the Individual — promoting respect and compassion for all individuals
- Personal Development — recognizing individuals who seek self-improvement.

Program objectives (covered in Chapter 2) should be "linking pins" for incorporating the mission, values, vision and operating philosophy into the recognition program. The program should mirror what the organization values as absolutely necessary for its continued success and growth.

Factor 4

Review current pay practices and rewards programs. All total rewards programs should be reviewed before implementing a recognition program. Some current programs may have some existing elements that can be incorporated into recognition. Figure 16 (Page 36) can be used to determine the key elements. After completing this checklist, it should identify the programs that should be incorporated into or replaced by a new recognition program.

Linking Recognition with the Performance Evaluation

Recognition should be an integral part of both the manager's and employee's performance evaluation. In this case, both the sender (i.e., generally the manager) and the receiver (i.e., the employee) should be evaluated on how well they are doing with the recognition process. Most managers have a review of essential leadership skills such as goal development, coaching, morale, communication and teambuilding. The review may include a statistical analysis that evaluates this year's performance against an identified standard. Other organizations discuss these leadership skills on a more open-ended basis by using a performance plan to discuss what it takes for the manager to be successful. Regardless of the method used, recognition should be at the top of the skill list when evaluating leaders.

Figure 17 (Page 38) provides a sample of how Major Corporation incorporates recognition into the performance process. This sample only illustrates one of the five key performance areas by which managers are evaluated. The other four areas are all impacted by employee recognition:

- Finances — How well the manager succeeds in keeping costs within budget and revenue at and above budget. Obviously, employees who feel valued will perform at higher levels, thus positively impacting the bottom line.

FIGURE 16: REVIEWING CURRENT PROGRAMS		
Type	**Program Features**	**Direct Linkage to Recognition**

COMPENSATION
  Base Salary
  Merit Increase
  Lump-Sum Increase
 	
  Group Incentive
 	
  Discretionary Bonus
	• Basic hourly or annual salary rate
	• Performance-based increase
	• Annual salary adjustment to those
	  individuals who have reached the
	  maximum salary rate.
	• Bonus provided to a work team
	  for completion of a project
	• Bonus to recognize exceptional
	  individual or group basis
		___YES ___NO
		___YES ___NO
		___YES ___NO
		
		___YES ___NO
		
		___YES ___NO

BENEFITS
  INCOME PROTECTION
    • Mandatory Programs
      Unemployment
      Workers' Compensation
      Social Security
    • Voluntary Programs
      Health
      Dental
      Vision
      Retirement
      Disability
      Flexible spending
      programs
	• Protects the standard of
	  living of the employee and his
	  or her family
		___YES ___NO

TIME OFF
  Paid Time Off
  Paid Breaks at Work
 	
WORK EXPERIENCE PROGRAMS
    Child Care
    Elder Care
    Employee Assistance
      Program
    Financial Planning
    Legal Assistance
    Flexible Scheduling
	• Provides income to the employee
	  (e.g., when the employee is not
	  working — vacation, sick and
	  holiday)
	• Addresses the individual needs of
	  the employee
		___YES ___NO
		
		___YES ___NO

- Quality — Does quality meet and exceed established standards? Employees have a direct impact on quality and should be rewarded when it is succeeded either individually or departmentally.
- Customer Service — Do we meet or exceed our customers' expectations? When customers compliment service, the employee or employees responsible should be rewarded and recognized.
- Change — How well does the manager deal with major changes and significant projects that impact the organization? Managers can use recognition to reward employees who embrace changes and contribute significantly to major departmental projects.

Any deficiencies by the leader in recognizing employee performance will be easily identified regardless of the evaluation method used. The point is not to have managers go through the motion of recognizing a given number of employees just to get a good performance review. The quality of the recognition is much more dramatic. If it is used appropriately, it can make a difference in individual and team performance. Recognition often is cited by employees on surveys as an important link to good work performance (i.e., Watson Wyatt's *What motivates top employees?*, Sibson/WorldatWork's *The Rewards of Work* and Hewitt Associates' *100 Best Companies to Work for in America*). It also is important to link the actual recognition with the employee's performance. Some employee performance tools are "criteria based" and can easily be linked with individual and team recognition. The following three performance areas can be linked to employee recognition:

- **Flexibility:** The employee's willingness to accept new work challenges and job assignments. A good recognition program looks at employee contribution. Obviously, a quality performer should be recognized for his/her ability to accept these challenges. Flexibility can be valued by directly recognizing the employee and providing more opportunity for that person to expand his/her role in the organization. Note: Work content was rated as the highest reward category by U.S. employees who participated in *The Rewards of Work* study conducted by Sibson/WorldatWork in 2000.
- **Customer Service:** The employee's ability to provide quality service to internal and external customers. This is an area that should be easily monitored using effective recognition techniques. Chapter 4 provides

FIGURE 17: LINKING RECOGNITION WITH MANAGERIAL PERFORMANCE

Key Performance Area: Leadership Skills
Factor Weight: 20%
Rating Scale: 1 — Does not consistently meet standards or projections
2 — Consistently meets standards or projections
3 — Exceeds standards or projections

Key Performance Monitor Rating	Basic Skill Definition	Methods of Measurement
Coaching	• Encourages employees to participate in problem-solving and quality-improvement activities	• Feedback from employees • Opinion survey improvement activities • Documented process improvements
Employee Recognition	• Consistently recognizes exceptional employee performance	• Number of documented employee recognitions during a specified period • Departmental morale • Departmental and organizational performance
Teambuilding	• Encourages teamwork within and between departments	• Feedback from employees and peers • Departmental performance monitors • Employee meetings, conducted at least monthly
Goal Development	• Clearly communicates goals, departmental needs and assignments with employees, peers, customers	• Feedback from employees • Feedback from customers and peers • Successful completion of goals and objectives
Communication	• Practices effective communication methods with employees, peers and customers	• Employee Opinion Survey • Peer feedback • Departmental surveys • Exit interviews with employees • Customer satisfaction surveys

a number of tools that can be used to recognize good customer service. For example, good service should be documented using basic techniques such as thank-you cards, congratulatory citations and gold cards that document excellent customer service on the spot. During the performance evaluation, any documented examples of good customer service should be cited and discussed. An absence of examples or negative feedback also should be discussed.

- **Team Relations:** This factor focuses on how well the employee cooperates with team members in completing departmental goals and projects. Both financial and nonfinancial recognition may have been provided for excellence in this area. It is important to reinforce recognition even if a financial reward was provided. Remember, the purpose of recognition is to reward positive work performance. The performance evaluation is another opportunity to again recognize this work contribution.

Recognition is actually another method for evaluating and rewarding positive work performance immediately rather than waiting for the performance evaluation to come around. The performance factors mentioned are not inclusive. In fact, good work in the areas of work quality, service delivery, safety, attendance, self-development and general attitude should be recognized and linked back to performance evaluation when it does eventually roll around.

Providing Feedback on Program Usage

Key stakeholders should be kept informed about how the program is doing. The three key stakeholders are employees, senior leadership and the board of directors. The best method for keeping employees informed is to provide a "Total Rewards Statement" to them at least annually. Figure 18 (Page 41) provides a sample statement. It is noteworthy that the total value of all total rewards programs is $72,307 compared to direct compensation of $43,000. The employee in Figure 18 earned $29,307 in additional value from programs provided in benefits (i.e., $22,707) and work experience (i.e., $6,600).

A "Summary of Program Usage" should be provided to senior leadership and to the board of directors. This summary should include the following key elements:

- Total number of employees recognized
- Program costs
- Impact on organizational morale, if known

- Impact on customer satisfaction
- Impact on productivity if it can be tied to recognition
- Impact on attraction, retention and employee development.

Figure 19 (Page 43) provides a handy pictorial for communicating the number of employees rewarded by a new spot recognition program. It indicates that the program was slow in developing, but gained steam in the last quarter of the year. This is a good trend that senior leaders and board members will appreciate. Figure 20 (Page 44) provides a sample program summary that can be used to communicate with senior leaders and board members. The key is to provide information that is easy to understand and communicate. The summary includes a rating scale that can be used by the recognition committee to assess the program's impact for the previous period (i.e., month, quarter or year). This assessment must be honest and supported by verifiable numbers or trends. It also is an excellent way to effectively communicate program success to key stakeholders.

The action plan column could be expanded in our sample usage report. The important point is this usage summary provides a quick and easy overview of all key program elements. This is the kind of qualitative information that key stakeholders want to see.

Linking Total Rewards with Attraction and Retention

All total rewards programs should be packaged together when attracting and retaining employees. The organization's attraction and retention plan should feature recognition. It is an element that can make a company stand out as unique and attractive. Program usage should be readily shared with applicants and employees. These numbers should in fact be prominently displayed on organizational bulletin boards and detailed in employee publications. Figure 21 (Page 45) identifies some prominent tools for discussing program content and usage with applicants and employees.

The checklist provides a variety of ways to get the recognition story to employees and applicants. Some are expensive (i.e., videos and total rewards fairs), while others are inexpensive (i.e., audiotapes, payroll stuffers and letters to the employee home) but may be equally effective. Choose the tools that best meet your employees' needs. Finally, the organization's attraction and retention plan should incorporate recognition by focusing on the following four issues:

Name: Joan Employee
Dates Covered: From: January 1, xxxx
                   To: December 31, xxxx

GENERAL STATEMENT:
The following is a summary of the value of the Total Rewards programs provided to you during xxxx. This is not intended to be an employment contract or a promise of future monetary payments to be paid by Major Corporation to any employee. It does provide a concise summary of the value of all Total Rewards. Please review this statement thoroughly to ensure you are familiar with all the programs detailed in this statement. Major Corporation is proud to provide these programs to its employees. Thank you for your many contributions during this past year.

_____
CEO Signature

I. COMPENSATION (Includes all direct and cash compensation provided to you in xxxx).

Direct Compensation for xxxx:	$40,000
Lump-Sum Bonus:	$3,000
Total Value of Compensation Programs:	$43,000

II. BENEFITS (Time off and income protection programs)

A. Time Off:

Paid Time Off (23 days)	$3,500
Paid Breaks (118.5 hours)	$2,250
B. Income Protection Plans:	$2,100
Social Security Contribution	$3,557
Disability	$500
Dental Plan (family plan)	$600
Vision Plan (family plan)	$200
Health Coverage (family plan at 75% paid by Major Corporation)	$4,500
Workers Compensation (cost per employee)	$500
Flexible Spending Program (day care)	$5,000
Total Value of Benefits Program	$22,707

III. WORK EXPERIENCE (Programs that address your individual needs)

A. Recognition Programs:	
Spot Recognition	$500
Cash Recognition (received March 18, xxxx)	$750
B. Work-Life Programs:	
Employee Assistance Program (family coverage)	$850
Financial Planning	$500
Legal Assistance	$400
Cafeteria Discount	$400
Convenience Service — on-site grocery	$300

(Continued on page 43)

1. What actions should be taken to reach a given attraction and retention target?
2. What outcomes should occur as a result of actions taken (e.g., lower turnover)?
3. What is the timeline established for completing the plan?
4. What is the plan's financial and organizational impact?

Integrate recognition into the attraction and retention plan as follows:

- Actions: Provide innovative recognition programs and approaches aimed at attracting and retaining quality employees.
- Outcomes: Coordinate recognition with all of the organization's total rewards programs to provide a competitive attraction and retention package.
- Timelines: Develop timelines in conjunction with other programs. New recognition approaches will have ongoing timelines and be customized to the organization's needs.
- Impact: The financial impact will be $450,000 for new recognition programs. All new efforts will be monitored for impact on attraction and retention. A market survey will be conducted to ensure that all total rewards programs meet the needs of employees and applicants.

As the market adjusts to the changing needs of job applicants, it is important to keep recognition programs competitive and fresh. A quick review of Hewitt's *100 Best Companies to Work for in America* reveals that these companies are not afraid to make changes and adapt to their employees' needs. This is an important lesson to learn if the organization is to use recognition as part of its attraction and retention strategy.

FIGURE 18: SAMPLE TOTAL REWARDS STATEMENT (CONTINUED)	
Shopping and Banking	$400
Elder Care	$600
Free Fitness Center Membership	$500
Service Awards Program	$400
Company-Provided Vacation Sites (free lodging near 4 major recreation areas)	$600
Employee Discounts on Company Merchandise	$400
Total Value of Work Experience Programs:	$6,600
TOTAL VALUE OF ALL TOTAL REWARDS PROGRAMS:	$72,307

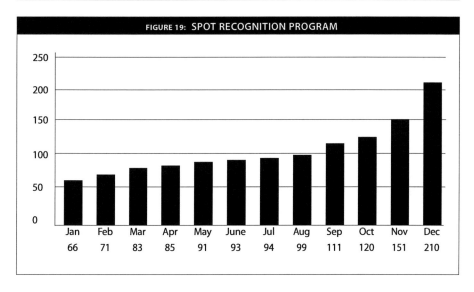

FIGURE 19: SPOT RECOGNITION PROGRAM

Jan	Feb	Mar	Apr	May	June	Jul	Aug	Sep	Oct	Nov	Dec
66	71	83	85	91	93	94	99	111	120	151	210

FIGURE 20: SUMMARY OF PROGRAM USAGE

Usage Period: Jan. 1 to Dec. 31, 2003

Ranking Scale: 1 — Program exceeds program expectations and projections
2 — Program meets program expectations and projections
3 — Program does not meet program expectations and projections

Key Program Element	Summary of Program Impact	Recognition Ranking	Committee Plan
Number of Employees Recognized	1,529 employees	2	Expand recognition to reach 1,800 employees for next year.
Program Costs	$450,000	2	Review cost of recognition program and determine areas that should be expanded.
Morale	Overall morale improved by 15% according to the latest opinion survey. The new recognition program was cited as a big reason for the improvement.	1	Continue to communicate the importance of recognition.
Customer Satisfaction	Customer satisfaction level remained the same at 82%.	3	Focus program on customer satisfaction and reach 90% level.
Productivity	Productivity increased 5% for the last quarter.	2	Recognize more team and departmental performance gains in the quarter.
Attraction, Retention and Development	Current vacancy rate is 5% compared to 12% last quarter. Employee turnover is below 10% compared to 18% for the last quarter. 21 employees were recognized for completing professional certifications.	1	Continue to emphasize recognition as an important tool for attraction, retention and development.

FIGURE 21: CHECKLIST OF KEY TOOLS USED TO LINK RECOGNITION WITH ATTRACTION AND RETENTION

___Internal Job Posting

___Job Postings on the Internet and Intranet

___Recruitment Advertisements

___Organizational Web Sites

___Organizational Newsletters

___Open Benefits Enrollments

___Internal Seminars and Workshops

___Career Fairs

___Recruitment Brochures

___Employee Handbooks

___New Employee Orientation

___Quarterly Forums with Administrative Staff

___Payroll Stuffers

___Letters Sent to the Employee's Home

___Attraction and Retention Videos

___Audiotape Summaries

___Information Sessions for Employees

___Total Rewards Fairs (which provide information about all total rewards programs)

___Total Rewards Statements

4

Selecting the Best
Recognition Alternatives

Authors Ken Blanchard and Sheldon Bowles provide words of wisdom in the book, *Gung Ho!* Regarding the importance of valuing and recognizing employees, the authors stated: "People who are truly in control work for organizations that value them as persons. Their thoughts, feelings, needs, and dreams are respected, listened to, and acted upon."

The key is to act upon what employees say they want in a recognition program. Selecting the right recognition alternative(s) is vital to the program's success. Some organizations choose to offer an expansive program that includes a number of ways to recognize employees. Other companies limit the scope and offer well-defined approaches to recognition. There really is no one best approach. According to author Bob Nelson, there are 1,001 ways to reward employees, and money is only one method. This chapter will explore how to select alternatives that best fit the organization's needs. The company's cultural needs and financial limitations restrict the number of desirable approaches.

Matching Program Goals and Organizational Culture

The four program objectives identified in Chapter 2 must be in concert with the organization's culture and employee relations climate. To determine if the goals and culture link effectively, employees should be asked what they think is important with regard to recognition. Figure 22 (Page 49) provides a sample questionnaire to solicit input. The questionnaire should determine what the employee and organization value as significant program outcomes.

Questions 1 and 3 were used to determine if the two major program objectives (i.e., Improving Employee Work Performance and Recognizing Excellent Customer Service) are really important to employees. Questions 2 and 6 ask for the type of recognition that employers should provide. This gives employees two opportunities to provide input about recognition techniques. It is noteworthy that employees are not asked directly until Question 7 if they want a recognition program at all. The first six questions allow us to determine plan design. The remaining four questions gather feedback in the following key areas:

- Employee support for a recognition program
- What performance areas should be included in the program
- Who is responsible for recognizing employees
- Best way(s) to communicate the program to employees.

Instructions: Please take time to carefully answer this questionnaire. The organization is in the process of developing a new employee recognition program for employees. Your input is vital to the program's success. Survey results will be posted on our Web site (www.MajorCorp.com) and on all bulletin boards throughout the organization. A survey summary also will be mailed to all employees. Thank you for your input and continued support of Major Corporation.

Some statements in the questionnaire should be answered by circling the number (i.e., 1, 2, 3, 4 or 5) that comes closest to your opinion about the statement:

1 = Strongly Disagree
2 = Disagree
3 = Neutral
4 = Agree
5 = Strongly Disagree

The other questions require a direct response from you. Please take time and give us your feedback on the open-ended questions.

Please mail completed questionnaires in the self-addressed envelope (attached). Again, thank you for your participation.

1. The organization does a good job of recognizing employees who exceed expected performance levels.

     1 2 3 4 5

2. What could the organization do to recognize employees who make significant contributions? Please elaborate:

_____
_____
_____

3. Excellent customer service should be rewarded and recognized by the organization.

     1 2 3 4 5

4. What types of positive customer behavior do you feel should be rewarded? Please elaborate:

_____
_____
_____

5. Management does a good job of recognizing employees for their contributions to the organization.

     1 2 3 4 5

6. Please rank the importance of each of the following in recognizing employees. The following is the ranking scale that should be used.

1 = Very Important
2 = Somewhat Important
3 = Not Important At All

Type of Recognition	Ranking of Importance		
Money	1	2	3
Time Off	1	2	3
Gift Certificate	1	2	3
Company Merchandise	1	2	3
Free Travel Getaways	1	2	3
Personal Thank-Yous	1	2	3
From Your Supervisor	1	2	3
Departmental Lunches	1	2	3
Fitness Center	1	2	3
Special Parking Places	1	2	3
Service Awards	1	2	3
Certificates of Recognition	1	2	3

Other Recognition Approaches (please elaborate):_____

_____
_____
_____

7. I believe the organization should develop and implement a recognition program to reward employees who make significant contributions.

    1   2   3   4   5

8. What types of work performance should this program recognize? Please elaborate:_____

_____
_____
_____

9. Who should recognize employees?

Senior Management	___Yes	___No
Department Directors	___Yes	___No
Supervisors	___Yes	___No
Co-Workers	___Yes	___No
Customers	___Yes	___No

Others (elaborate):
_____

10. What is the best way to communicate the program to employees? Check all that apply:

    ___Letter sent to the employee's home
    ___Payroll stuffers
    ___Internet
    ___Intranet
    ___Department meetings
    ___General employee sessions
    ___Recognition hotline
    ___Other methods:

Once survey results have been tabulated, it is important to benchmark the data with what other similar organizations are doing in the area of recognition. Benchmark data is extremely helpful in determining the criteria to include in the program. For example, when Major Corporation benchmarked survey data with other competitors, it found the following parallels:

- First-line supervisors were the program drivers and provided most of the recognition to employees.
- Paid time off was an extremely popular method of recognition with competitor employees.
- Employees prefer cash to softer items such as gift certificates and thank-you cards.
- Employees in other organizations preferred general information sessions to introduce the program.

The above data can easily be obtained from human resources departments, and comparative data from professional associations such as WorldatWork. There also is published survey data on the Internet. The important point is to make use of all available data in making the selection decision. Employees also will ask the proverbial question: "How do our competitors recognize their employees for outstanding contributions?" If at all possible, the organization needs to be prepared with an appropriate response to how it compares with other organizations.

Finally, benchmark data provides concrete examples of how a program can be designed. For example, the above benchmark data along with other survey data indicates that first-line supervisors are key to program success. It also suggests that employees prefer cash or cash-related methods for being recognized. This data is valuable in determining the types of programs to offer.

One important reminder is that the best source of data remains the feedback received from the organization's own employees. They will tell the company what is important to them.

Program Design

Figure 23 (Page 53) details different program features that can be used in the design of a recognition program. These program features are broken into two major categories:

- Programs Linked Directly with Other Total Rewards Programs — These formal programs are represented in the top half of Figure 23. Formal programs are geared toward long-term recognition and have established criteria and monitors. Some characteristics include the following:
  - Direct link to the performance evaluation system
  - More administrative oversight required
  - Substantial cost investment
  - Generally ongoing and seen as more objective by employees.

- Programs Focused on Immediate (or Spot) Recognition — These informal programs are represented in the bottom half of Figure 23. Informal programs aim at immediate results and have fewer guidelines and requirements. Some identified characteristics include the following:
  - Less training and communication required
  - Less administrative oversight
  - Less program investment
  - Short-term in nature and viewed as more subjective by employees.

When designing either type of program, it is essential that the organization determine which features it wants to support and to what degree. As stated previously, a company can have more than one approach to recognition. Both categories represented in Figure 23 can be the basis to develop formal and informal recognition programs. The intent is to recognize and motivate employees. One approach to recognition will not work for everyone. Every employee has different needs and preferences when it comes to recognition.

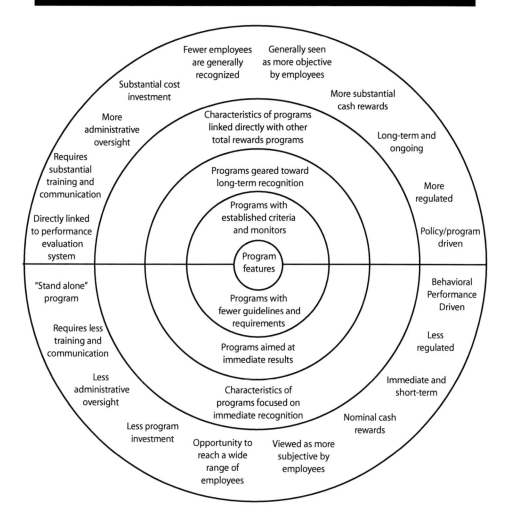

The organization must attempt to align employee needs and preferences when designing its program.

Formal Recognition Programs

According to Bob Nelson, author of *1001 Ways To Reward Employees,* formal recognition programs can simply be defined as a "predetermined program." But a formal recognition program is not only predetermined, but also an integral part of the total rewards program. It involves the organization making a long-term commitment to recognition. Formal programs must be well communicated and understood by all key stakeholders. Communicating their intent and merit to employees is key to their success. The intent must be to reward and recognize employees for their personal achievements and contributions. The program also should be seen by employees as more than the "feel good" program of the month. It must stand on its merit as an important management tool. Figure 24 (Page 56) details the essential elements of a formal recognition program.

Cash vs. Non-Cash Programs

One essential element of a formal recognition program as identified in Figure 24 was to offer rewards that are meaningful and provide either financial or personal value. Formal programs can meet these criteria by utilizing both cash and non-cash rewards. Figure 25 (Page 57) provides examples of programs that employ both cash and non-cash recognition.

Figure 25 provides a partial list of available approaches. Additional recognition approaches also are discussed in the section on informal recognition programs. Some formal approaches discussed as "non-cash approaches" in Figure 25 also can be utilized in an informal program depending on the criteria applied. The major point is that a formal recognition program should be flexible enough to address employee needs. Some employees want public recognition, and many of the non-cash approaches provide this need at little or no cost.

Designing a Formal Program

Step 1 — Establish monetary and program boundaries. It is important to keep the recognition meaningful, but also stay within established program boundaries. Some program boundaries include the following:

- Recognition only will be given for performance considered over and above established standards (e.g., excellent customer service).
- Cash bonuses will not exceed $500 for any one recognition event.
- The program will not duplicate any current total rewards programs (i.e., cash compensation, employee benefits or related work experience program).

Step 2 — Identify the behavior/performance to be recognized.
This was addressed in Step 1, but needs to be reinforced. Eligible behavior may include the following:

- Performance/behavior that exceeds normal expectations
- Behavior that exceeds the supervisor's expectations
- Action(s) or behavior that enhance(s) the organization's image
- Action(s) or behavior that delight(s) the customer
- Improved work process or a new approach to work problems.

Step 3 — Determine who does the recognizing. A decision matrix (See Figure 58) can be developed as a guide. It designates the individuals directly or indirectly involved in the recognition process.

Customers and co-workers can provide non-cash recognition (e.g., certificate of recognition) if the organization feels this is appropriate. In some companies, the recognition committee presents all cash awards to track the money spent and to provide more public recognition.

Step 4 — Develop guidelines for communicating recognition to employees. Some basic guidelines for communicating the actual recognition should be developed. These guidelines provide leaders with a tool similar to "talking points." Leaders should use talking points to announce the recognition program to employees. The communication guidelines are useful in structuring the recognition itself. Some sample communication guidelines follow:

- Inform the employee, if permissible, who nominated him/her for recognition (e.g., co-workers, customers, supervisory observation, etc.).
- Provide a detailed description of the actual achievement or contribution. Example: "You provided excellent customer service to Mr. X. You patiently listened to his requests and responded in a timely and professional manner. You also provided product information immediately. I appreciate how you handled this situation."
- Cite the performance standard or work process where the employee exceeded expectations.

- Links Recognition with the Achievement
    - Recognizes and rewards specific achievements such as improvements in work processes
    - Recognizes significant individual and group contributions
- Widely Communicated
    - The program is communicated to all key stakeholders on an ongoing basis.
- Well-Defined Program Criteria
    - Has specific criteria for granting recognition
    - Identifies specific behavior/performance to be recognized
- Encourages Employee Involvement
    - Employee input is actively solicited.
    - Employees may participate in developing program goals.
- Employs Meaningful Rewards
    - Establishes rewards that have significant dollar or personal value
    - Designs rewards that mirror what employees have identified as important
- Rewards Group or Team Accomplishments
    - Incentives given to teams for significant contributions
    - Establishes a framework for rewarding group efforts for specific improvements in work processes
- Clear Monitors are in Place to Link Recognition and Achievement
    - Well-defined monitors determine areas of ongoing success.
    - Monitors are used to communicate program progress to key stakeholders.

The last essential element is *linking recognition to the performance evaluation*. This can be accomplished by doing the following:
- Documenting the Recognition
    - This can be placed in the employee's personnel file, or a separate recognition file can be maintained.
- Linking the Recognition with a Specific Performance Area
    - For example, if the recognition is for excellent customer service, this should be linked with the customer-service goals established on the performance evaluation tool.
- Establishing Recognition Standards
    - If the leader and the employee have already established key performance standards, these standards should be integrated with the recognition.
    - For example, the following performance standard is integrated with recognition (Note: The Recognition Standard is in bold type):

Employees will be rewarded when **customer expectations are exceeded by 10 percent**, as measured by the customer satisfaction survey. The customer satisfaction survey is administered to all customers at the completion of the service provided by each individual employee or work team.

The example is called a "complex standard" because it incorporates elements of performance and recognition. Where possible, leaders should integrate performance and recognition into the evaluation system.

FIGURE 25: EXAMPLES OF FORMAL RECOGNITION APPROACHES			
Cash Approaches	**Cash Advantages**	**Non-cash Approaches**	**Non-cash Advantages**
Cash Bonuses	Can be tied to specific achievement	Service Award	Has trophy value and long-term recognition value
Paid Time Off	Easy to administer, and employees view it as extra pay	Employee of the Month	Provides public recognition
Stock Ownership	Can be tied into other total rewards programs	Certificate of Recognition	Provides personal value to the employee
Paid Travel	Builds excitement and fun	Flexible Work Schedules	Allows employee to build work schedule around his/her needs
Gift Certificates	Low dollar value and easy to administer	Telecommuting	Allows employee to work at home
Recruitment Bonus	Employees help recruit new employees	Company Merchandise	Aligns with the company
Educational Grants	Depending on plan, can provide educational scholarships to the employee's family	Reserved Parking	Provides public recognition

- Document the recognition if possible.
- Select an appropriate place and time to communicate recognition. Note: The best time to communicate recognition is at the beginning of the employee's work shift. The recognition will positively impact the individual for the entire workday. Also, some employees do not want to be recognized publicly. Sometimes, the best place to recognize them is behind closed doors.
- Be prepared to answer questions and discuss the recognition in detail with the employee. Note: Giving your time is an important part of the recognition process.

Step 5 — Document the recognition with a "congratulatory citation." The congratulatory citation can be placed in the employee's personnel file and linked with the employee's performance evaluation. It details what took place, the person involved in the achievement, how the individual was successful, when the action occurred and where it happened.

Step 6 — Establish guidelines for reinforcing positive behavior and desired performance. (See Figure 27, Page 60.)

Informal Recognition Programs

Informal or spot recognition rewards employees immediately for making positive contributions. It is a program that is relatively easy to implement, and training time is minimal for participants. There are seven essential elements of a spot recognition program (See Figure 28, Page 61):

1. Financial limits should be established before the program is implemented. Note: Dollar limits are generally low, and in some cases non-cash awards are used exclusively.

2. Establish who has the ultimate responsibility for administering the program (i.e., human resources department, recognition committee, program coordinator, etc.).

3. Develop a clear definition of the program that can be widely communicated and easily understood.

4. Establish who is eligible to participate in the program.

FIGURE 26: DECISION MATRIX			
Non-cash Recognition	**Cash Recognition**	**Cash Recognition**	**Cash Recognition**
	$400 - $500	$200 - $399	Less Than $200
Senior Leadership	Chief Executive Officer	Department Director	Supervisor/Manager
Department Director	Administrative Staff	Vice President	Senior Leaders
Board Members	Supervisor	Department Director	Work Leader
Recognition Committee	Recognition Committee	Recognition Committee	Customers Co-workers

5. Identify what actions, behaviors and performance areas will qualify for spot recognition.

6. Identify exclusions if appropriate.

7. Establish the procedures and guidelines that will be used to recognize an individual.

Spot recognition is unique because it has elements that fit with both a formal and informal program. It provides immediate recognition much like an informal program but still has definitive structure like a formal program. Figure 28 provides an example of the "Star Card" spot recognition program that combines both cash and non-cash rewards in an easy to administer format. The Star Card program guidelines are presented as follows:

- Star Cards are given to employees who provide excellent service to customers, visitors and fellow employees. Some examples of "star service" include, but are not limited to, the following:
    - Promptly responding to customer concerns and questions

    - Displaying extraordinary customer relations skills according to feedback received from customers

    - Exhibiting positive team skills that support the work group and the organization's goals

    - Going above and beyond the call of duty in delivering quality service as observed by the customer, employee's supervisor or a co-worker.
- The supervisor or leader will give the Star Card on the spot to the employee who has exceeded customer service standards.
- Employees who receive a Star Card can return the card to HR to be eligible for a monthly prize drawing worth $500.
- After the monthly drawing is held, the Star Card is returned to the supervisor, who will use it when preparing the employee's performance evaluation.
- The star card program provides an inventive method of taking a simple spot recognition program and building excitement while focusing on the critical goal of customer service. This program is a "win-win" for the organization, the employee and the supervisor.

- Document the positive behavior or performance.
- Establish performance and recognition standards and communicate them to employees.
- Talk about recognition at department meetings, in memorandums and on Internet/intranet sites. Let employees know how important positive behavior and performance are to the organization.
- Leave something tangible with the employee (i.e., cash or non-cash award).
- Conduct the recognition as close to the desired performance as possible.
- Provide a detailed explanation to the employee of the desired behavior/performance.
- Revisit the positive achievement to reinforce to the employee the performance's importance. This also tells employees that positive contributions are remembered and valued by the supervisor and organization.
- Refer to the recognition when conducting the performance evaluation to reinforce the importance of positive contributions.
- Solicit employee input about the recognition process and what behavior/performance should be rewarded.

Designing an Informal Program

Informal recognition programs are less structured and spontaneous in nature. They often are referred to as "in the moment" programs that reward positive actions and behavior as they occur. Effective informal programs should still be planned so the recognition can be meaningful and meet the employee's needs.

Step 1 — Define the program's purpose. This does not have to be a complicated defined purpose but should state simply what the program is trying to accomplish. For example: "The purpose of the informal recognition program is to recognize employee actions that can be readily observed and immediately rewarded."

Step 2 — Determine who will be eligible. Generally, all employees are eligible to participate in an informal recognition program. Administrative staff and possibly department directors usually are the two groups of individuals excluded. Other organizations also exclude temporary, casual and contracted employees from the program. Since informal recognition is relatively inexpensive, it is a good idea to include as many individuals in the program as possible.

Step 3 — Establish program expectations. The expectations should be built around areas that the organization is seeking to improve. Examples include customer service, organizational morale, team development, productivity and personal development. The following expectations are an example and are not as well defined or developed as what is generally seen in a formal recognition program.

Policy Statement: It is a policy of Major Corporation to provide a program to immediately reward individuals (or employees) who exceed expected performance levels or who provide exceptional customer service. The recognition committee is responsible for coordinating the spot recognition program.

Purpose: The purpose of the spot recognition program is to reward employees immediately. The monetary value of spot recognition awards is less than $25.

Definition: Employees will be recognized for meaningful contributions that exceed expected levels of performance, which are detailed in the employee's job description and/or the employee's performance evaluation. Spot recognition should be timely and immediate and encourage similar performance or behavior in the future.

Eligibility: Administrative staff and department directors are not eligible for spot recognition. All other employees and supervisors are eligible for the program.

Eligible Actions/Behavior: The following guidelines should be used to determine if the performance or behavior qualifies for spot recognition:

• The employee's performance exceeded normal expectations for the job.
• The employee's action(s) or behavior(s) enhanced the organization's image.
• The employee's action(s) or behavior(s) delighted a customer.
• The employee's action(s) or behavior(s) exceeded the supervisor's expectations.
• The employee's action(s) or behavior(s) exhibited an entrepreneurial/intrapreneurial spirit in resolving a problem or handling a customer concern.

Exclusions: 1. If the employee is already being compensated or rewarded for the performance or effort, the employee will not be eligible for spot recognition (i.e., an employee who agrees to work an alternate work shift and receives additional compensation for working the shift). 2. The employee performs a duty that is expected or that is not beyond normal work expectations. An example would be directing a customer to the appropriate office for service.

Program Guidelines: 1. Any employee can nominate or recommend another employee for spot recognition. The recommendation can be presented to the employee's supervisor or to a member of the recognition committee. 2. A customer also can recommend an employee for spot recognition. 3. The supervisor/leader will present the recognition to the employee. 4. If possible, the recognition should be documented and sent to the human resources department for inclusion in the employee's personnel file. 5. Items that can be used for spot recognition can be obtained from HR.

- Increase management visibility with employees and provide them a tool to reward positive work performance.
- Provide a positive work environment that recognizes employees for their contributions.
- Gratify employees who will feel good about their work and contributions.
- Recognize those employees who provide exceptional customer service.
- Encourage similar performance by the employee in the future.
- Recognize those employees who provide meaningful contributions to the organization.

Step 4 — Define what behavior and actions are eligible for recognition. An informal program should not be a "giveaway program" that gives "stuff" to employees who make meaningless contributions. Although it is a spontaneous program, leaders need to focus on meaningful contributions. The following bullet points are the types of behavior and actions that would warrant special attention. The difference between these behaviors and those listed in the spot recognition policy is that managers still have some discretion when using an informal approach to recognition.

- The behavior or action resulted in a compliment from an internal or external customer.
- The employee exceeds expectations on a project or work assignment.
- The employee displays an unusual, cooperative spirit in working with other team members or with other work areas.
- The employee's actions enhance the organization's image.
- The manager/supervisor observes the employee engaging in actions that will improve morale or enhance the organization's image.
- The employee goes above and beyond the call of duty without being asked to do so.
- The employee makes a work improvement or changes a process that will increase productivity or efficiency.
- At the supervisor's discretion, any action that in her/his estimation adds significant value to the organization should be recognized.

The last identified action is to provide flexibility to the supervisor when using an informal approach. There is no exhaustive list that can identify all eligible performance areas. Using an informal approach allows the supervisor to recognize those performance areas that do not fit neatly into a formal program.

Step 5 — Identify the types of recognition approaches to be used. Most informal programs use small cash awards, recognition certificates, merchandise or some other token(s) that employees value. Janis Allen, author of *I Saw What You Did and I Know Who You Are,* advocates having employees complete a "reinforcer survey" to determine what things they would like to see in the program. This is a good idea as long as the program's original purpose and intent is not distorted with meaningless or extravagant recognition items.

The following award items are a representative example of what often is found in an informal program:

- Thank-you card from the supervisor
- Gift certificates
- Small cash bonuses (generally less than $50)
- Movie tickets
- Video rental certificates
- Lunch with the supervisor
- Weekend trips
- Flowers or balloon bouquets
- Team dinner
- Free parking spot
- Full or partial day off with pay
- Articles in the employee newsletter
- Personal recognition from the CEO
- Manager publicly recognizes the employee in a department meeting
- Celebration lunches or dinners at the work site.

It is important to identify what can be given to the employee. Some organizations believe in a limited list while others have hundreds of items available. Regardless, supervisors and leaders need to know what is available and how to use it for recognition.

Step 6 — Match informal approaches to the organization's culture. The recognition should reflect what is important to the organization's culture.

For example, if the culture is mature and conservative, a more traditional approach such as certificates of appreciation and cash awards may be more appropriate. In younger, hip organizations, departmental parties, gift certificates and other types of public recognition may be needed. Use the cultural audit discussed in Chapter 2 to determine what works best for the company. Be careful to also monitor the culture of the department or work team, which may be significantly different than the organization's culture. The supervisor should identify those unique characteristics present in his/her work area and work with the recognition committee to build an effective recognition program.

How to Effectively Use an Informal Program

An informal recognition program must effectively align with the organization's business strategy. This only happens when the recognition efforts are built on trust and credibility. Informal programs can be severely impacted if they become an approach used on a "hit and miss" basis. They should be consistently applied and continuously communicated to employees. Informal recognition programs have five basic principles:

- Acknowledge and recognize employees in a timely manner, using specific and concrete examples of the positive performance. Employees want to know what they did right. They also want to receive recognition in conjunction with the contribution. This adds value to the employee and to the achievement.
- Bridge the recognition with organizational goals and business strategy. If the recognition is not focused on the company, it will appear disjointed and unimportant to participants. The message to employees should be that the organization values their contributions and wants them to be a partner in meeting goals. For example, excellent customer service is often a focal point for the company. When employees are recognized for good customer relations skills, it emphasizes that customer service is valued and appreciated by the organization.
- Center the program on the organization's culture and values. As discussed previously, this means matching recognition with the culture.
- Develop positive performance skills in employees by recognizing their achievements. The recognition should reinforce positive work behavior.
- Enlist support from all program participants. The recognition should focus on how to keep the program meaningful and still meet the needs of all participants.

These principles provide a foundation from which to administer a successful program. There also are some obstacles to avoid. Figure 29 on Page 67 details some obstacles to avoid if the program is to be taken seriously by employees and other key stakeholders.

Keeping the Program Fresh and Fun

To keep enthusiasm high about the program, it must adapt to the changing needs of the participants. Many of the companies listed in *Fortune's* "100 Best Companies to Work For" incorporate fun and uniqueness into their recognition efforts. Some of these companies incorporate recognition with other total rewards programs to address specific needs not often considered. It includes building recognition around work/life issues. Some programs, like the Star Card example, have both formal and informal approaches to recognition. All of these programs have one consistent theme: "Our programs focus on the individual and his/her unique needs and desires." Some of the following examples may seem unconventional but are effective nonetheless:

- Someone walking the employee's dog during work
- Hand-addressing Christmas cards for the employee
- Settling billing disputes with a dry cleaner
- Providing on-site university courses
- Flexible work schedules to meet the employee's needs
- On-site fitness centers
- Putting greens
- Free fruit to employees
- Convenience services on site including banking, dry cleaning, hairdresser, masseur, car wash
- Free snacks
- Daily popcorn parties
- Valet parking services
- Company pools where employees can swim and relax during work hours
- Casual dress built around various themes (i.e., Hawaiian, '50s, '60s, country, etc.).

Some programs go beyond the scope of what a traditional recognition program generally offers, but this is why employees value those companies. The recognition committee needs to survey employees and supervisors at least annually to determine what can be done to keep the program fresh. The individuals doing the recognition also should be recognized for their willingness to reward others in the organization. This also keeps the supervisor/leader excited about and committed to the program's success. The following four suggestions should help keep the program fun and exciting:

- Add new recognition components at least annually if possible. For example, let employees have time off to attend a school function for their children.
- Tailor the recognition to meet the employee's unique needs.
- Think outside the box. What's wrong with casual Thursdays every so often?
- Celebrate! Recognition comes alive when we celebrate the individual and group achievements of our employees.

Conducting the Recognition Event

According to Ken Blanchard and Spencer Johnson in the *One-Minute Manager*, "You can never over recognize, the more you recognize people, the more productive they'll be." If this is true, why do so many leaders avoid recognizing employees? The problem is that leaders are uncomfortable telling employees that they did a good job. The recognition event is the cornerstone of the recognition process. The leader must be fully prepared when communicating praise to the employee. Figure 30 (Page 68) should be used to plan and communicate the recognition to the employee.

If at all possible, the recognition should be done face-to-face by the supervisor/leader. In this electronic age, some leaders like to use the Internet and e-mail to recognize employees. The recognition's impact may be less in those cases. Some of the guidelines in Figure 30 would still apply for electronic recognition. The key is to personalize the praise and use active verbs to indicate excitement and enthusiasm to the reader. After completing the recognition event, document it along with the specific achievement.

Documenting Recognition

A well-documented recognition event helps the leader link it with the employee's performance evaluation. The documentation also is important to employees when they are seeking a promotion or job transfer. An individual who has a history of being recognized as an outstanding performer will have an easier chance of moving up in the organization. Documented recognition (See Figure 31 on

69) reinforces and encourages the employee to repeat his/her outstanding performance. It is a template for employees to use for future work behavior.

The most difficult task is focusing on specifics when documenting the recognition. Figure 32 (Page 69) gives a few examples of how to be specific when recognizing employees. Documentation should avoid general statements about the achievement and instead use specific facts when describing the event.

FIGURE 29: PROGRAM OBSTACLES

- Inconsistent and infrequent application of the program
- Failure to match the reward with the achievement
- Failure to adapt the recognition to the individual's preferences
- Poor communication by the supervisor/leader with the employee
- Person doing the recognition has a low level of trust and credibility with employees
- No clear definition of what actions/behaviors are being recognized
- Lack of understanding by participants of what the program is trying to accomplish
- Failure to communicate tax implications of some rewards
- Inadequate time allotted by the supervisor/leader when recognizing the individual
- Failure to keep the program fresh and fun
- Lack of enthusiasm for the program by participants.

These obstacles should be addressed up front before the program is allowed to stall. The last two obstacles must be carefully scrutinized since those two are often responsible for the program's long-term failure.

- Select an Appropriate Time and Place
  - Individual meeting: Use this approach when the employee does not like public recognition.
  - Departmental meeting or group setting: Use this approach to publicly celebrate the recognition.
  - Hold the meeting at the beginning of the workday. This allows the employee to feel good all day.
  - Allow enough time to appropriately recognize the employee.
  - Recognition should be as immediate as possible.
  - Avoid negative locations when conducting the recognition. Some examples include the supervisor's office, the employee's work area or a public location.

- Document the Recognition if Possible
  - Use a congratulatory citation, thank-you card or certificate of recognition.

- Communicate the Recognition Brightly and Clearly
  - Choose positive statements to communicate the recognition (i.e., "I appreciate the long hours and quality of work you put into this project," as opposed to, "This certainly was better than the last project you were assigned").
  - Use nonverbal cues that positively reinforce the recognition.
  - Maintain eye contact with the individual.
  - Use positive facial expressions such as smiling to indicate approval.
  - Use an open body stance.
  - Warmly greet the individual with a firm handshake.
  - Use a voice tone that communicates positive reinforcement.
  - Avoid sighing and long periods of silence.
  - Maintain a moderate pitch level.

- Be Specific About the Achievement
  - Provide clear and specific facts and examples of why the individual is being recognized.

- Encourage Input from the Employee

- Leave Something Tangible with the Employee
  - Thank-you card
  - Gift certificate
  - Cash award.

FIGURE 31: GUIDELINES FOR DOCUMENTING RECOGNITION

_____Focus on specifics.

_____Cite the performance standard or organization goal that was exceeded, if appropriate.

_____Describe in detail the achievement.
- Who was involved? List the names and individuals involved.
- What happened? Describe exactly what the employee achieved that was extraordinary.
- When did the achievement occur?
- Where did the achievement occur?
- Why is this event being recognized (i.e., exceeds a departmental goal, an example of exceptional customer service)?

_____Include comments of appreciation by the individual giving the recognition in the documentation.

_____Document the date the recognition was given.

_____Indicate the type of recognition approach used, if appropriate.

_____Provide a copy of the documentation to the employee.

_____Place a copy of the recognition in the employee's personnel file.

FIGURE 32: BE SPECIFIC WHEN RECOGNIZING EMPLOYEES

General Statement	Specific Fact
Your performance has been excellent lately.	Mary has exceeded the transcription standard by 15% during the six-week period ending Oct. 1, XXXX. Her line count was up a total of 1,200 during this same period.
You have good customer relations skills.	On Sept. 8, XXXX, John Smith assisted a customer in locating a hearing aid. The customer lost the hearing aid in the dining room area. John also assisted the customer in obtaining batteries for the hearing aid. John transported the customer during his off duty hours to obtain the batteries.
You are an outstanding team member.	Sharon conducted research for a group project during her day off. She also arranged a site visit for her work team to benchmark the change before it was implemented.

5

Preparing an Action Plan

Once the decision has been made to offer a recognition program to employees, the next step is to develop an action plan. This plan details the actions and resources necessary to implement successful recognition efforts. It provides a map for the organization to ensure all aspects of the program have been identified. The plan also is a working document that may need to be modified to accommodate organizational needs.

Generally, the program coordinator, in conjunction with the recognition committee, is responsible for drafting the plan and submitting it to senior leadership for approval. The action plan should be discussed at length with all key stakeholders to ensure it has organizational support. Once approved by senior leadership, it should be widely communicated with employees and input solicited. While completing the action plan within the identified timetable is important, it is more important that the organization implement a worthwhile program. Each area in the plan is equally important and must be addressed before implementing recognition efforts.

Figure 33 (Page 73) details the dimensions that should be included in an action plan. Some of these dimensions will entail additional planning, which may necessitate a stand-alone plan complete with additional resources.

The six dimensions detailed in Figure 33 can be used to build the action plan. As each dimension is expanded, it is essential to identify specific human and capital resources.

How to Identify Resources

To determine resource needs, there are three questions to consider:

- Who needs to be involved in implementing and designing the program?
- What capital resources need to be committed to the program?
- How is the program going to be implemented and communicated?

The first question should focus on the financial and time commitments for the individuals involved directly in implementing the program. This involves more than a simple key stakeholder analysis to determine the players needed. Some people may not be key stakeholders once the program is executed. A program player is any internal or external individual directly involved in design and implementation. Some external players disappear or have minimal involvement once the recognition efforts are in place.

FIGURE 33: DIMENSION CHECKLIST FOR AN ACTION PLAN		
Dimension	**Key Components**	**Responsible Party**
Human	Input From Key Stakeholders	Recognition Committee/ Program Coordinator
	Training of Key Stakeholders	Program Trainers
	Surveying Employees	Program Coordinator
	Consultant Cost If Necessary	Program Coordinator/ Chief Financial Officer
Capital	Recognition Awards	Senior Leadership
	General Program Design	Recognition Committee
	General Program Costs	Program Coordinator
Administrative	Policy Review	Program Coordinator
	Developing Guidelines	Recognition Committee
	Designing Infrastructure	Senior Leadership
	Designing Training Program	Program Trainers
	Ongoing Administration	Program Coordinator
Data Collection	Organizational Assessment	Program Coordinator
	Surveying Employees	Program Coordinator
	Monitoring Program Usage	Department Directors
	Benchmarking Program	Program Coordinator/Senior Leadership
Legal	Plan Design	Program Coordinator
	IRS Compliance	Legal Consultants
	Tax Implications	Tax Consultant
	Reporting Requirements	Legal Consultants
Communication	Communication Plan	Program Coordinator
	Communicating To Key Stakeholders	Recognition Committee Senior Leadership/
	Feedback from Employees	Program Coordinator
	Announcing The Program	Recognition Committee
	Training Key Stakeholders	Program Trainers
	Ongoing Communication	Program Coordinator/ Senior Leadership

The second question is contingent upon what type of program the organization chooses to implement. Chapter 1 identified capital resources common to most programs. Figure 33 detailed three key components of the capital dimension:

- **Recognition awards** — The direct cost of the cash and non-cash awards granted to employees.

- **General program design** — The cost of designing the program, including all necessary training materials.
- **General program costs** — The overhead costs associated with the daily operations of the program.

These three key components are impacted by how the program is going to be implemented and communicated. If it is informal and focused on recognizing employees occasionally, the overhead costs may be minimal. If it is committed to reaching as many individuals as possible and includes formal guidelines and goals, the communication and implementation costs will be much more significant. Figure 34 (Page 76) uses the above three questions to develop a resource checklist of what capital and human resources will be needed for the program. Figure 34 also identifies some human and capital resources for the six dimensions discussed in Figure 33.

Establishing A Timetable

The last step in developing the plan is establishing a timetable for completing each critical program area. A good rule when establishing a timetable is to allow about six months to fully develop and communicate the program. Figure 35 (Page 77) provides some proposed timelines for each of the five program areas.

Some of the timelines can run concurrently with key elements such as the readiness assessment and the cultural audit. These two elements can run simultaneously to reduce the time it takes to implement the program. Timelines should be established very judiciously to fully develop and communicate the program. A big reason that recognition plans fail is that not enough thought and time were given to developing an effective program in the first place. It is essential that all participants understand why the recognition plan is being offered. If the supervisor shows up handing out gift certificates with little notice or explanation, the long-term impact on employee performance will be minimal. It takes time to build a program that fully communicates that recognition is an integral part of work life.

Putting It All Together

It's now time to complete the action plan. The plan will include action steps that address the five critical program areas. It also will incorporate the six essential dimensions throughout the plan. Finally, it will include a timetable.

The action plan and the previously developed budget are important tools for monitoring and implementing the program. The communication area is so vital to the program's success that a separate plan will need to be developed and will be discussed in Chapter 7.

Figure 36 (Page 78) provides a comprehensive action plan. Remember that this is a working document and can be changed if needed. The plan ties actions and resources together so program planning can be facilitated. The key stakeholders and players have already been identified previously via a separate analysis. This analysis can be used to complete the "Human Resources" section of the plan. The section on "Data/Financial Resources" includes the categories of capital and technology resources that will be needed for each action step. This section will not include any dollar amounts because these resources should already be included in the program budget. The sample action plan in Figure 36 has 11 steps built around the critical program areas. Each step provides a general overview of what will be needed to address that critical area. The completed plan is the final blueprint for implementing recognition efforts. The organization must take this blueprint and use it to carefully craft a successful program. This means the company must commit time, money and resources if the program is to become an integral part of the employee's total rewards package.

FIGURE 34: RESOURCE CHECKLIST		
Resource Question Needed	**Key Plan Dimension**	**Resources**
Who needs to be involved? Coordinator Leadership Committee Consultants Resources staff	Human Administrative	___Employees ___Program ___Senior ___Recognition ___Customers ___Supervisors ___Outside ___Program coordinator ___Payroll department ___Office space ___Office supplies
What capital resources need to be committed?	Capital	___Cash and non-cash awards ___Costs for program design ___Overhead costs for operating the program ___Computers and equipment needs
How is the program going to be designed, implemented and communicated?	Legal Data Collection Communications	___Legal consultants ___Accounting support ___Resource publications ___IRS guidelines ___Software ___Computer hardware ___Systems support from internal information management department ___Survey questionnaire designed internally or externally ___Outside consultants ___Employee focus groups ___Study groups ___Marketing department ___Printed brochures and program supplies ___Video if used ___Intranet and Internet posting of program ___Audio cassette if appropriate ___Presentation materials ___Outside trainers if used

Program Area	Key Elements	Suggested Timeline
	FIGURE 35: PROPOSED TIMELINES	
Assessment	Readiness Assessment	7 to 10 days
	Cultural Audit	7 to 10 days (concurrent with the readiness assessment)
	Surveying employees	21 to 30 days
Program Integration	Developing a program budget	10 to 14 days
	Integrating with other total rewards programs	14 to 21 days
Program Design	Selecting program features	30 to 60 days
	Finalizing program guidelines	30 to 60 days (concurrent with selecting features)
Monitoring	Legal compliance review	10 to 14 days
	Data collection	14 to 21 days
	Developing scorecard	7 to 10 days
	Developing program indicators	7 to 10 days and ongoing
Communication	Communicating the program	30 to 60 days
	Training participants	30 to 60 days (concurrent with communicating the program)

	FIGURE 36: SAMPLE ACTION PLAN		
CRITICAL PROGRAM AREA	**ACTION STEP(S)**	**HUMAN RESOURCES**	**DATA/ FINANCIAL RESOURCES**
ASSESSMENT	1. Assessing the organizational readiness	• Key stakeholders • Employees • Program coordinator • Senior leadership • Human resources staff • Recognition committee	• Readiness assessment • Cultural audit • Consultant cost
	2. Surveying employees	• Employees • Program coordinator • Key stakeholders • Outside consultant	• Employee focus groups • Consultant cost • Survey questionnaire • Software • Systems support
PROGRAM DEVELOPMENT	3. Selecting recognition alternatives	• Program coordinator • Payroll department • Human resources staff • Recognition committee • Outside consultant	• Benchmark data • Consultant cost • Supply and equipment cost • Software cost • Cost of non-cash and cash awards
	4. Reviewing current total rewards policies and developing new policies as needed	• Human resources staff • Payroll department • Program coordinator • Recognition committee	• Software • Outside consultant cost • Staff cost for review
	5. Designing program infrastructure	• Recognition committee • Program coordinator • Senior leadership • Department directors	• Consultant cost • Equipment and supply costs • Legal consultants • Staffing costs for recognition staff • Program objectives
PROGRAM INTEGRATION	6. Developing a program budget	• Program coordinator • Chief financial officer or designer • Senior leadership • Department directors	• Benchmark data • Program costs • Software • Supplies and equipment • Marketing and printing costs • Administrative costs

GOALS/MONITORS	7/01	7/15	8/01	8/15	9/01	9/15	10/01	10/15	11/01	11/15	12/01	12/15	01/01
• Establish organizational commitment to employee recognition.	7/01-7/11												
• Obtain employee feedback about program needs. • Use data to help design recognition program.		7/12-8/12											
• Select and design the recognition program that will be offered to employees.				8/12-9/20									
• Develop policies and guidelines for the program. • Review existing policies and procedures.				8/13-9/20									
• Establish a framework from which to administer the program. • Develop objectives for the program .				8/13-9/20									
• Establish a budget from which the program can be administered.						9/21-10/05							

CRITICAL PROGRAM	ACTION STEP(S)	HUMAN RESOURCES	DATA/ FINANCIAL RESOURCES
PROGRAM INTEGRATION	7. Integrating with other total rewards programs	• Program coordinator • Human resources staff • Payroll staff • Recognition committee • Senior leadership	• Total rewards budget • Productivity measures • Program objectives
MONITORING	8. Reviewing tax and legal requirements	• Legal consultant • Financial services department • Tax attorney • Program coordinator • Senior leadership	• IRS guidelines • State and federal guideline • Tax codes • Cost of legal review
	9. Developing program monitors and indica-tors	• Program coordinator • Recognition committee • Senior leadership • Department directors • Outside consultants	• Benchmark data • Program scorecard • Software cost • Consultant cost • Recognition survey • Cost of survey data
COMMUNICATION	10. Communicating program to all key stakeholders, including training all program partici-pants	• Program coordinator • Recognition committee • Marketing representative • Senior leadership • Department directors • Supervisors • Program trainers • Employees	• Printed brochures • Program supplies • Intranet/Internet • Media costs (i.e. video, audi cassette) • Salary costs for employees to come to information sessions
	11. Implementing the recognition pro-gram	• Program coordinator • Recognition committee • Senior leadership • Managers and supervisors • Employees	• Ongoing program costs • Printing and marketing costs for program kickoff

GOALS/ MONITORS	7/01	7/15	8/01	8/15	9/01	9/15	10/01	10/15	11/01	11/15	12/01	12/15	01/01
• Integrate recognition into the total rewards structure.							10/06-10/17						
• Ensure program complies with all legal and tax regulations.								10/20-10/30					
• Develop measurement tools for determining program effectiveness.									10/31-11/15				
• Develop and implement a step-by-step approach to communicating the program. • Provide training to all employees and key stakeholders.										11/16-12/30			
• Provide a recognition program that is an integral part of the organization's total rewards program. • Note: This is the last action step and represents the program's effective date.													01/01

6

Training Leaders

Chapter 2 identified the program coordinator as the individual directly responsible for developing a training program for leaders and employees. This individual will need to select a group of key employees who will assist with recognition training efforts. The trainers should possess the following skills/attributes:

- **Excellent facilitator skills:** Trainers will be facilitating rather than training. "Hands-on" exercises should be used in place of lectures or other traditional classroom training techniques.
- **Patient listening skills:** Trainers need to have the ability to listen patiently and completely answer questions about the program.
- **Highly credible and visible:** Leaders and employees should see trainers as trustworthy. The individual also should be someone high profile who is visible throughout the organization.
- **Committed to recognition:** The individual should be highly vocal, supportive and strongly committed to recognition as an important management tool.

Who meets the criteria of a trainer? Generally, long-term department directors and supervisors meet some or all of the criteria. Opinion leaders, who are individuals widely respected throughout the organization, also are excellent resources as trainers. The more the individual is respected and believed by the audience, the easier it will be to train him/her. Once the training team is in place, the next step is to establish learning objectives. These are different than the program objectives discussed in Chapter 2. Learning objectives determine how leaders are going to be trained about recognition. A training program can be developed and conducting through the following learning objectives:

- **Program Content**
  - All leaders in the organization are trained on program content, including basic eligibility criteria.
  - Training is linked to program objectives.
  - Program expectations are discussed and feedback solicited from organizational leaders.
- **Conducting the Recognition Event**
  - Leaders are trained on how to recognize and reinforce positive work performance.
  - Leaders are trained on how to document positive work behavior.

- Recognition is linked with effective communication skills.
- Recognition guidelines are developed and integrated into the program.

- **Creating Team Synergy**
-   Training is focused on creating value for the work team and recognizing group accomplishments.
- Individual and group strengths are identified and communicated by the leader.
- Individual and group recognition are linked together to create a balanced management tool.

- **Tracking Performance**
-   Recognition standards are developed and integrated into the program.
-   Effective monitoring techniques are discussed and implemented in each department/work unit.

- **Taking Responsibility**
-   Leaders are responsible for rewarding positive work contributions.
-   Leaders become fully responsible for the program's success.
-   Employee recognition is linked with leader performance and organizational expectations.

- **Ongoing Commitment**
-   Leaders attend at least one follow-up training session every quarter.
-   Leaders develop and implement individual goals to accomplish effective employee recognition.
-   Leaders share recognition successes on an ongoing basis with other leaders in the organization.

Some organizations choose to use outside consultants to train leaders. If used, the organization should establish specific guidelines to be followed by the outside trainer. Learning objectives should be developed in conjunction with the consultant. A member of senior management should introduce any training session conducted by an outside person. This lends credibility to the process. The bottom line is to keep senior management fully involved in the process even if an outside consultant or inside training source is used.

Ongoing Training Approaches

Follow-up training with leaders is essential if the program is to be successful. Ongoing training keeps the program a priority. The follow-up sessions can be less than an hour in duration and should focus on successes and novel approaches to recognition. This adds enthusiasm and builds program support. Reunion meetings with all leaders should be conducted for at least four hours annually. The purpose is to identify current recognition techniques and share how the program has impacted the organization. Depending on the topics covered, the company also can offer continuing education credits for attending a reunion meeting. To build initial confidence, all leaders should be provided "talking points" that can be used when recognizing employees or discussing the program. Talking points are mini-scripts provided to leaders so that consistent themes and messages will be sent to employees and other key stakeholders. Figure 37 (Page 87) provides a list of sample talking points.

The talking points are built around answering the why, what, who, how and when. These five traditional questions can be used to build an excellent script for leaders to use when telling employees about the program. Organizations with a number of different locations may want to add another traditional question: Where? Employees in remote locations will want to know if the program affects them or is just for employees in the main office. Talking points will need to be updated to reflect the current program. The quarterly follow-up sessions offer the perfect venue for soliciting input from leaders regarding what needs to be added to or deleted from the talking points.

Providing Recognition to Leaders Who Complete Training

A sample certification program with five modules is presented in Figure 38 (Page 89). This program is approximately 12 to 16 hours of "hands-on" training. It involves a major financial investment by the organization. However, if it is to be successful, it is essential to invest the time and money it takes to effectively train leaders. When the program is completed, the organization can present an internal certification to the leader who finishes all five modules. This designation could be "certified recognition leader" to send a message to other leaders that recognition management is important to the company. The program also addresses crucial management areas such as

Why is this program being offered now?

- "The organization is committed to rewarding and recognizing positive contributions made by employees."
- "This program provides all employees an opportunity to be recognized for their individual and group contributions."
- "Employees expressed on the recent Employee Opinion Survey that their contributions often go unnoticed by management."
- "This program will make us more competitive in attracting and retaining employees."
- "We believe our employees deserve more attention for providing excellent customer service."

What is being offered to employees?

- A combination of monetary and nonmonetary methods will be offered to employees. The list includes the following:
- Cash bonuses
- Time off with pay
- Gift certificates
- Personalized recognition from the supervisor
- Paid weekend getaways
- More challenging work assignments and possible promotions for positive work contributions.

What are the program's objectives?

- To provide a program to reward employees who exceed expected performance levels by at least 10 percent
- To recognize employees who have made meaningful contributions to customer service
- To create a more satisfying work environment for employees
- To provide a program that aligns with all the other total rewards programs (i.e., compensation and benefits)
- To reduce employee turnover by at least 20 percent
- To reduce the job vacancy rate by at least 5 percent.

How will the program be communicated to employees?

- Individual meetings will be held.
- "I have exciting news regarding your work environment."
- "The organization is committed to providing a positive work environment that rewards and recognizes employees who make positive contributions."
- "We believe this program will make us more competitive when recruiting new employees."
- "We listened to our employees who asked for more recognition for positive work performance from their supervisor on the last Employee Opinion Survey."
- "This program provides managers with an opportunity to immediately reward employees for excellent customer service and positive work performance."

- A letter from the CEO announcing the new program is sent to the employee's home.
- General informational sessions are held.
- General sessions lasting approximately one hour will explain the program in detail will be provided to all employees on all work shifts.
- General sessions will be videotaped and used during new employee orientation and for those employees who are unable to attend.
- General sessions will be offered on cassette tape for blind employees and translated into the native language of our global associates.
- An Internet/intranet link will be provided.
- Employees can access program information on the organization's Web site and intranet.

Who is affected?
- All employees, full- and part-time, will be eligible for this program.

When will the new program become effective?
- The program becomes effective on Sept. 1, XXXX.

communication, performance management, teambuilding and statistical monitoring.

Figure 39 (Page 90) links the training with leader performance. The first three areas (change management, basic leadership skills and employee development) are traditional for most leaders. When recognition management is added to the performance expectations, it results in making the leader more valuable to the organization. Leaders who are committed to recognition management should be financially rewarded for their efforts by the company. Completion of the certification program should become an expectation by the organization and senior leadership. There should be a graduation ceremony, and the CEO or designated senior leader should be present to give each graduate a certificate of completion. Graduates also should receive recognition such as a gift certificate or a celebration luncheon with the graduates. Certification should be widely publicized by senior leadership and become a prerequisite for being considered for future promotions. In short, completion of the training program should be seen as something the organization values and encourages. The certification also sends a positive message to employees, who now see that their leaders are committed to effectively recognizing and communicating with them.

Module 1: Recognition Management

• Program content
• Conducting the recognition event
• How to effectively reward

Module 2: Documentation Recognition

• How to effectively document positive work performance
• Linking recognition with the employee performance evaluation

Module 3: Basic Communication Skills

• Verbal communication
• Counseling employees
• Feedback/technique
• Effective listening skills

Module 4: Team Recognition Strategies

• Creating team synergy
• Group recognition techniques
• Motivating teams

Module 5: Tracking Program Performance

• Developing recognition standards
• Effective monitoring techniques
• Developing a recognition scorecard

FIGURE 39: LINKING TRAINING WITH LEADER PERFORMANCE

Chance Management
• Implemented new
program changes

+

Basic Leadership Skills
• Financial/management
• Project development
• Quality control
• Customer service
• Employee relations

Employee Development
• Coaching
• Performance management
• Goal setting

+

Recognition Management
• Completed recognition
program
• Developed recognition
standards

=

CERTIFIED RECOGNITION LEADER (CRL)

7

Communicating During Implementation

Communication is the key element to the recognition program's success. At this point in the program's development, a step-by-step communication plan should be developed. It should be used in conjunction with the action plan to identify what steps are needed to communicate and implement the program (these were the last two action plan steps). The communication plan focuses on these steps and provides a systematic approach to address them. The following steps are essential to building an effective plan:

Step 1 — Answer the following key questions before establishing a plan:
- Who will be affected?
- What is going to be communicated (e.g., a formal program, cash versus non-cash awards, the recognition process, tax and legal implications, etc.)?
- Where are the stakeholders located who need to know about the program (e.g., multiple locations, all work shifts, specific departments, specific geographic areas, etc.)?
- When do employees and other key stakeholders need to know the information?
- Why do employees and stakeholders need to be informed (i.e., there is a new component of the total rewards program)? Unless the organization appropriately communicates the program to employees and key stakeholders, it will never be seen as an integral part of the total rewards program.
- How will the organization communicate the program to employees and key stakeholders?

There are a number of media and activity-based approaches. Media approaches range from brochures to videos. There will be more discussion later about the effective use of media. Activity-based approaches include training and employee meetings, which allow the employee and stakeholder to get actively involved in the learning process.

Role playing and interactive learning sessions are tools sometimes used to get the participants involved in learning about the program.

Step 2 — Identify steps that must be taken to communicate the recognition program.

Examples

- Develop the program's theme.
- Solicit input from key stakeholders about program communication.
- Identify key messages to send to stakeholders about the program. Examples include: "We want to recognize employees for giving extraordinary service to our customers." "Employee recognition is an important part of the total rewards program."
- Develop program brochures and other communication approaches.
- Train leaders about the program.
- Send program announcements to all key stakeholders.
- Conduct meetings with employees.

Step 3 — Identify action(s) to take.

Examples

- Work with the marketing department to develop a program theme.
- Conduct focus group(s) with key stakeholders to develop communication approaches.
- Review key program messages with senior leadership.
- Work with the marketing department and outside printing sources to develop program brochures.
- Establish a training program for organizational leaders.
- Send letters to all key stakeholders announcing the program's implementation.
- Meet with employees on all shifts and at all locations to provide program information.

Step 4 — Establish expected outcomes.

Examples

- Solicit input and support for the program.
- Provide detailed information to key stakeholders.
- Implement a new employee recognition program.

Step 5 — Identify the resources needed. Some resources already were identified in the action plan. It is important to identify specific resources needed for communicating and implementing the program.

Step 6 — Establish a timetable for completing the communication process.

Communication Objectives

The following objectives focus on program communication and are different than the program objectives.

- Inform all eligible employees about a new recognition program.
- Increase awareness of the new recognition program with at least 85 percent of all eligible employees.
- Train all management staff about the program and how to effectively recognize employees.
- Meet with all eligible employees to communicate the program and the process to be used for recognition.
- Obtain at least a 75 percent acceptance of the new program from all eligible employees.

Key messages then should be developed to link program content with the communication objectives. These messages also are invaluable in developing program themes and sending consistent information about the program to key stakeholders. Key messages should be few in numbers and really focus on what is important:

- Employee recognition is an integral part of the total rewards program.
- We want to recognize our employees when they give extraordinary customer service.
- The recognition program rewards employees for positive work achievements.
- The recognition program provides a wide range of awards.

With objectives and key messages developed, the audience for the communication should be identified. This should be relatively easy because most key stakeholders should have been identified in the first two steps of the action plan, when the organizational readiness was assessed. The remaining audience for communication may include vendors, employees' family members and site coordinators, if there are multiple locations. The timetable for completing the plan can range from 45 to 90 days depending on the size of the organization.

Using Internal Resources

The recognition team was discussed in Chapter 2 as the program's chief architects and torchbearers. This team is vital to the program's implementation and communication. At this stage, the recognition team must become a formal, standing committee. As a committee, these key individuals need to sell the program to employees.

At this point, informal leaders should be included in the committee's structure. Informal leaders are well respected by employees and will break down barriers during the communication and implementation process. The recognition committee should have structure and defined term limits. It should be an honor to serve on it. The committee should have input and a direct line to the program coordinator. If a formal recognition program is adopted, this group should review and recommend for approval to senior leadership the program's guidelines and rewards structure. Figure 40 (Page 96) defines the essential functions of a recognition committee. These functions may be more defined in a larger organization.

Serving as a sounding board to the program coordinator and senior leadership is perhaps the most meaningful contribution that the committee can make during the implementation process. A good recognition committee can help leadership avoid problems before they occur because it knows the culture and the pulse of the organization. Because of the respect level that these committee members generally have with employees, they will know what works and what doesn't work regarding program communication. Some members also can be used as program trainers if time commitments allow. The bottom line is this should not be a dormant committee but an active force in the implementation and communication process.

Other internal sources include in-house individuals who have good teaching skills. These people can be used as program trainers. Again, these individuals should be committed to the recognition program. If the HR director is not the program coordinator, this person or an HR designer needs to be actively involved in the implementation and communication process. Finally, train individuals to serve as facilitators for focus groups or data collection. This saves consultant dollars and can lend credibility to the feedback process if highly respected people are chosen.

Employee Feedback

Focus groups are an excellent way to solicit feedback from employees and can obtain data from a cross-section of employees. The best use of the focus group is to gather critical feedback on how to effectively roll out the recogni-

FIGURE 40: ESSENTIAL FUNCTIONS OF A RECOGNITION COMMITTEE	
Essential Function	**Scope of Responsibility**
Serves as a sounding board.	Serves in an advisory capacity to the program coordinator and senior leadership.
Reviews and recommends changes as necessary to the communication and implementation strategies plan.	Reviews all communication to ensure content matches program objectives.
Participates in the selection of media approaches.	Reviews all media alternatives and makes suggestions about what works best with employees.
Participates in developing the program theme.	Ensures program theme and corresponding key messages link with program and communication objectives.
Solicits feedback from key stakeholders	Seeks input about how widely the program is understood and accepted.
Participates in developing training programs for leaders.	Reviews training programs to determine if leaders are prepared to effectively recognize employees.
Remains highly visible in the organization during the program's announcement and implementation.	Shows active support of the program by being available to answer questions and display enthusiasm about the program content.
Attends and participates in employee meetings.	Lends credibility to the program by having a member of the recognition committee present at meetings.
Assists in evaluating the program.	Works with the program coordinator to assess the effectiveness of the program and how well it was communicated.
Arbitrates program concerns and issues.	Serves as an objective source in hearing and resolving program concerns.

tion program. For example, ask the group, "What do you feel is most important to communicate to employees about the recognition program?" Feedback from this and other questions should generate some useful ideas on how to effectively communicate and implement the program.

The biggest problem often encountered with focus groups is the failure to structure them appropriately. The following are guidelines for using a focus group for employee feedback:

- Keep the groups small, limiting them to 10 to 12 employees.

- Select the employees randomly using statistical sampling techniques (i.e., use a statistical software program to select employees by department, unit, location or shift).
- Do not put supervisors and their subordinates in the same focus group.
- Make every effort to have cross-functional groups. This avoids having one department or work area dominate the discussion.
- Do not use "subject matter experts" to lead the groups. These individuals will dominate the discussion and attempt to narrow the feedback.
- Allow the group to provide open-ended feedback rather than focusing on just "yes" or "no" responses.
- Provide an atmosphere that encourages open feedback and critical discussion.
- Avoid giving feedback to the participants while the group is in session. It is important to listen and absorb what the individuals are saying.
- Provide a general overview of the topic to be discussed but avoid training the participants about the subject.

Electronic brainstorming is another tool that can be used with some degree of success. It allows employees to provide confidential feedback in a small group setting. It differs from a focus group because the employee is giving feedback via the computer terminal. The group leader coordinates that data at a master terminal and feeds it back to the group for further input. Each round of electronic brainstorming builds on data received confidentially from each group member. This avoids having one or two members dominate discussion. It also can be structured so each person provides some feedback on the topic. The downside is that some individuals are still intimidated by computer technology. Additionally, some organizations cannot afford to offer this as a feedback tool.

Conducting open forums with employees to provide general program information is also an excellent tool for soliciting feedback. Information sessions should be structured, or they become gripe sessions or "talking head presentations." A talking head is someone who gives a boring program overview in an unemotional and uncaring manner. Such presentations kill the enthusiasm that participants may have otherwise generated from an interactive and exciting delivery. The following are guidelines for conducting employee information sessions:

- Use individuals who have excellent facilitating and speaking skills to conduct the session.
- Develop and use a program agenda to keep the session focused.
- Offer the session(s) at times that are convenient to the participants (e.g., second and third shifts).
- Widely communicate the times and locations of the sessions.
- Keep the session to no more than 60 minutes in length. Most individuals lose focus and interest after 60 minutes unless there is a break.
- Create fun and excitement during the session to encourage participation and program support. This can be accomplished with a quick, fun exercise about the program that energizes the participants.
- Offer specific examples of how the program will recognize employees.
- Save time for questions and answers at the end of the session.
- Post recurring questions and answers on the intranet or on bulletin boards throughout the organization.
- Establish a central contact person or place if employees want to provide additional feedback.

Information sessions should be kept moving to reach the maximum impact on employees. This involves blending the need to provide information with the ability to give employees an opportunity to respond. The above guidelines should help the right facilitator keep the session on track.

Communicating with Multiple Locations and Global Cultures

Communicating with employees in multiple locations can be difficult, even given the current electronic technology. No matter the communication technique ultimately used, it still must convey the key messages and program objectives. Employee recognition is difficult for some employees to absorb and understand; this is exacerbated when the organization has multiple locations with vastly different cultures. The following guidelines should be used when communicating recognition to multiple locations:

- Identify one individual responsible for coordinating the communication effort for that location. This could be a trusted informal leader or the human resources representative for that location. It is essential that employees at the location highly trust and respect the individual.

- Establish a confidential source for the individual to ask questions of or give input to (e.g., a dedicated e-mail address, telephone hotline, private fax, program coordinator or recognition committee member).
- Use language familiar to the individuals working in that location or geographic area. For example, de minimis benefits certainly would need more explanation for most employees. Formula-based programs also will need much more in-depth communication. Avoid using colloquialism when communicating the program (e.g., "We want to recognize those employees who hide their talents under a bushel"). These sometimes can offend and alienate employees.
- Avoid novel communication approaches that may offend employees. Examples include communication approaches that poke fun at the local community; communication that implies that employees in this particular location are difficult or slow to learn; communication that talks down to employees; and communication that fails to take into consideration the cultural differences of the employees.
- Coordinate communication to be released to all locations at the same time. This ensures that all employees receive the same information. It also prevents the grapevine from being the communication network of choice. Sometimes, the grapevine can produce destructive and inaccurate results. It is best to provide an equal communication effort at all locations if possible.
- If possible, assess the effectiveness of the communication with employees. Techniques such as short surveys on the intranet, follow-up memorandums, conference calls and focus groups can be useful in assessing communication efforts.

When communicating with employees in different global cultures, the biggest challenge is to offer communication that provides uniform understanding. Some helpful hints when communicating with employees in different global cultures include:

- Use a language expert to check any written memorandums before sending them to employees. Also, use a language expert to review other media materials such as videos, audio or slide presentations. This will help avoid communication errors with employees.
- Make sure there is a clear understanding of the cultural differences to

ensure the communication does not offend the receiver. Again, a language expert can lend some expertise in this area. It could be embarrassing if the program objectives and key messages are at odds with the employee's value system.

- Determine the expectations of the employees in the other global cultures. Money and energy can be wasted if the program fails to meet their expectations.
- Do not assume expertise is uniform across cultures. For example, some formal recognition approaches may be difficult to explain to individuals who are not used to being rewarded beyond the traditional paycheck.
- Avoid using humor or other novel communication approaches that may be difficult for the employee to understand. In fact, some humor may offend employees in other global cultures.
- Use a language expert to design and present, if possible, any verbal communication programs. The literal translation is extremely important when communicating verbally with employees. The audio cassette is an excellent tool. A language expert can present material on the audio cassette to repeatedly send an accurate and consistent message.
- Identify a contact person who will help coordinate the communication and answer any follow-up questions from employees. The contact person should be an individual who is well-respected by employees in that global culture. This individual should have expertise about the culture and obviously be able to communicate to employees in their native language.

Recognizing and honoring their differences is the best approach when communicating with employees in multiple locations or different global cultures. Organizations often are guilty of creating communication geared toward one audience. What works in Boston may not work in Brussels or Atlanta. Site coordinators at these other locations should play a vital role in the communication process, helping to assess what works well in their location or culture. Communication then can be tailored to meet the needs and unique demands of all employees in the organization.

Using Media-Based Approaches

A combination of several different media approaches should be used, if possible, when communicating the new program. For example, a memorandum giving program details should precede any formal meetings with employees. Or, employees can attend a video training session in various locations to accommodate their schedules. The bottom line is that there are many media choices. However, the media used must complement the message being sent. It should never overwhelm the audience.

With so many media alternatives available, how can the organization determine what to select? Figure 41 (Page 103) lists the most common media sources and ways to effectively use them. Cost and turnaround-time are two important elements in selecting media. The least expensive method probably is a general memorandum that details the program to all employees, but employees often fail to read memorandums or letters sent to them. This is why other approaches are needed. Communicating the program is equivalent to marketing a new service or product. The same thought must be put into selecting the appropriate media. The organization should be marketing recognition as an important part of the total rewards program. If the intent is to use an informal program aimed at spontaneous recognition, with rewards that have a de minimis value, there is less need for a major marketing effort. However, most recognition programs are more complex and should be appropriately communicated. Printed materials are the best source for documenting program content and can be used to communicate to a wide audience. Some printed media also must be developed for training and for communication. Most other sources must be supplemented with printed materials. In selecting media, the organization should answer the following questions:

- **What type of media sources will best communicate the program to employees?** In some organizations, video presentations or other gimmick communication approaches turn off employees. Video presentations can be seen as expensive and taking money away from the program. Other employee groups feel they add excitement to the communication effort. The intranet/Internet also represents varying degrees of challenge for the organization. Younger employees are tuned in to technology and prefer communication electronically. More mature employees sometimes resist using newer technology and may even view it as impersonal. The bottom line is to know what works best for your employees before selecting a media source.
- **How much is the organization willing to spend communicating the**

program? Some organizations are willing to spend a great deal communicating a new recognition program because it represents a major cultural change. In this instance, the organization may be willing to invest in videos, elaborate audio-visual programs and even a standalone Web site geared only to employee recognition. If the organization wants to keep costs down, a more modest approach will be used. In this case, activity-based communication efforts that include employee meetings with presentations using basic overheads could be utilized. Some organizations will invest little or no money in media, preferring instead to surprise the employee with the recognition. The only problem with this approach is that recognition never becomes fully integrated in the total rewards program. It becomes a standalone program never fully understood or appreciated by employees. If it is to have lasting impact, individuals must see it as important to their work environment. This only will be accomplished if employees understand and value the program.

- **How much time is the organization willing to invest in the process?** Some media can take a significant amount of time to develop (e.g., videos, handbooks, audio-visual techniques and specialized Web sites). If the organization wants a quick turnaround time, it should select media sources that are easy to develop and produce (e.g., memorandums, payroll stuffers, flyers, short audio presentations and overheads). It is important to remember that media development affects the timetable. If the media takes longer to produce, the communication plan should be revised and coordinated along with the original action plan.

- **Who are the audiences for the communication effort?** If the organization is attempting to communicate with a wide audience, printed materials will be essential, along with the Internet and some audio-visual techniques. If the program is going to be used as a recruitment tool, a video may be an excellent way to capture an applicant's attention. Recognition is a major element applicants focus on when deciding which organization values its employees the most. If the communication effort's purpose is to inform and enlighten, the company may want to use more traditional methods such as program summaries, informational flyers and letters to the employee's homes.

			COST			TURN-AROUND

FIGURE 41: COMMON MEDIA SOURCES

MEDIA SOURCE	EFFECTIVE USES	EXAMPLES	1 Low	2 Medium	3 High	TURN-AROUND TIME TO COMPLETE
PRINT	• Conveys complex and detailed information • Reaches a wide audience • Can be used in conjunction with other media • Provides a written reference source • Excellent resource for training • Can generate program interest with a wide range of individuals	• Memorandum	X			1 week
		• Letters to employees	X			1-2 weeks
		• Handbook	X	X	X	6-8 weeks
		• Program summary description	X	X		2-4 weeks
		• Brochures		X	X	6-8 weeks
		• Payroll stuffers	X	X		2-3 weeks
		• Informational flyers	X	X		1-2 weeks
VIDEO	• Excellent source for training • Conveys factual and emotional content • Provides a visual presentation to communicate program • Can be used to provide testimonials by senior leaders to support program • Can be used individually, or in large or small groups • Should be used in conjunction with printed media	• Major video production developed by an outside source		X		6-12 weeks
		• In-house production using leaders and employees		X		6-8 weeks
		• Small video clips offering testimonials or small bits of program information		X		4-6 weeks
AUDIO-VISUAL	• Provides consistent message • Should be used with other media • Provides a structured presentation • Can be used with small to large audiences • Conveys factual data and emotional content EFFECTIVE USES	• Narrated slide presentations		X		6-10 weeks
		• Speaker leads presentations with visual examples		X		6-12 weeks

MEDIA SOURCE		EXAMPLES	COST			TURN-AROUND
			1 Low	2 Medium	3 High	TIME TO COMPLETE
AUDIO VISUAL	• Provides a visual application of the program • Provides opportunity for involvement by the recognition committee	• Program summaries tied to printed materials		X		4-6 weeks
AUDIO CASSETTE	• Provides literal translation to global and vision-impaired employees • Can reach a wide audience • Relatively inexpensive to produce • Can be used effectively with printed materials	• Audio cassette that provides complete program information	X	X		4-6 weeks
		• Short audio presentations to generate program interest	X			2-4 weeks
INTRANET/ INTERNET	• Can be excellent source for organizations with multiple locations • Provides factual information • Can be interactive and allow participants to comment about the recognition program • Geared to the modern employee who values technology • Reaches a wide audience • Can provide graphical representation	• Organizational Web sites		X	X	6-12 weeks
		• Intranet communication networks		X	X	Varies
		• E-mail	X	X		1-2 weeks if in place
GENERAL COMMUNICATION TOOLS	• Can be used to present the program to employees • Can be used in conjunction with other media • Can be customized to the audience or location • Facilitates discussion and interaction	• Slide presentations		X		4-6 weeks
		• CD-ROM		X	X	6-8 weeks
		• Overheads or other software presentation approaches (e.g. Power Point)	X	X		1-2 weeks

FIGURE 41: COMMON MEDIA SOURCES (CONTINUED)

- **Does the media overpower the intended message?** Some media sources may overpower the program's intended message. For example, brochures that also incorporate public relations and marketing approaches may detract from employee recognition. The intent of the media should be to communicate the recognition program in a simple but creative manner. Media that has static statements from senior leadership about profit levels and the importance of employee performance or media that uses complex formulas and difficult-to-understand words often will turn off employees. Videos may be overkill for a program geared to spontaneous recognition. On the other hand, a video or audio-visual presentation may actually enhance a formal safety recognition or cash bonus program. The ultimate objective should be to choose a media source that complements the message and ties it to the program's basic theme.

- **Does the media create excitement about and support for the recognition program?** In short, does the media build momentum and employee support? There are a number of media sources that build excitement and anticipation. Depending on the culture, payroll stuffers, colorful flyers and brochures, audiocassettes and creative intranet/Internet sites can be used to build enthusiasm for the program. Figure 42 (Page 108) provides a sample payroll stuffer/flyer that can be used as a communication teaser to give basic information about the program without giving all of the details. A teaser always is used in conjunction with other media sources. In fact, it informs the reader that additional information is to follow. Because some organizations have direct payroll deposit, the teaser also could be an informational flyer distributed to employees in departmental meetings or on intranet sites. The purpose is to build interest in and excitement about the program.

The audio cassette is another good source for building excitement. It can be used to provide a complete and literal translation of the program or to provide short "bites of information." These short bites can be creative and entice employees to learn more about the recognition efforts. For organizations that incorporate technology in their communication, Internet/intranet media can provide creative approaches to communicating recognition. Creative approaches such as online surveys, fun graphics and checklists all can be used to effectively communicate the program.

In some cases, it is preferable to use an outside consultant to select and design the media. Keep in mind that using outside consultants can increase program costs and, in some cases, increase the time it takes to implement the program. The best use of consultants is to have them create difficult media (e.g., major videos) and review the overall communication plan.

Informing Customers and the Community

An important implementation strategy is to inform the organization's customers and the surrounding community about the program. The purpose of the communication is twofold:

- **To enhance the public relations image of the organization.** Customers and the overall community look favorably on organizations that recognize their employees for significant achievements. The communication should focus on how the company values its employees and how recognition sets it apart from other businesses. It also should be an announcement rather than a detailed analysis of the program content. The announcement is an opportunity to showcase the organization as a caring, positive place to work and do business.
- **To directly involve customers and the public in the recognition process.** The communication should ask customers and the public to recommend those employees who perform extraordinary service. This is an excellent way to involve customers. It also sends the message that the organization cares what they think. The best way to involve others is to have a process by which employees can be recommended for recognition. One approach is simply to have customers fill out an appreciation card that can be presented directly to the employee. The card also can be used as the basis for additional recognition by the organization.

Because the communication is a public announcement, the following sources should be used:

- **Newspaper/magazine advertisements.** The announcement can appear as a standalone announcement paid for by the organization in an area newspaper or regional magazine. It should be an oversized announcement that highlights the program's purpose and the reason(s) the organization has the program.

- **Internet/Web site postings.** The program can be featured on the organization's Web site for the public to view and make comments on.
- **Public announcements.** Depending on cost, radio spots can be used to announce the program to the public.
- **Informational flyers and brochures.** These can be presented to customers as they come to the organization. A supply also can be provided to local chamber of commerce offices. Send a mailing to current customers informing them about the program.
- **On-site program posters and other posted notices.** It is important that the notices be large enough to catch the customers' and public's attention.

The following sample announcement can be used to communicate the program to the public:

Major Corporation Announces a New Recognition Program for Its Employees

This is to announce a new and exciting program that will be provided to our employees. Major Corporation is committed to providing them a positive work environment. We believe employees who feel good about what they do will provide better service to our customers. Major Corporation is offering a new recognition program that recognizes and rewards those workers/staffers who provide extraordinary service to our customers and the organization. We ask for your help in identifying those employees who deserve recognition for their contributions. If you notice an employee providing excellent service to a customer, or making a positive contribution to our organization, please let us know. We have appreciation cards available at all Major Corporation locations. These cards can be completed on any employee who makes a positive contribution. Cards can be mailed to Major Corporation or dropped in a recognition box located in the lobby of all our locations. We also encourage anyone to visit our Web site at majorcorp.xyz.org to make recommendations. Thank you for participating in this important process.

Major Corporation strives to support its customers and employees and continue to create an atmosphere that promotes loyalty, integrity and service. Thank you for your support in this important endeavor. We believe all our employees are committed to excellent service and outstanding performance.

The above announcement can be adapted to a variety of media (e.g., the Internet, posters, flyers and general public announcements). The more the public is aware of the program, the more customers will reinforce it to employees. This gives workers increased program awareness as they seek to be recognized for excellent customer service. It also builds customer and employee loyalty because the organization is seen as committed to providing a positive work environment.

Theme-Related Events

Conducting a theme-related event on site is one way to build fun and excitement about employee recognition. This event should focus solely on praising the employee. One such approach is to conduct a recognition fair that showcases the new program in a creative manner. Figure 43 (Page 111) provides some essential elements of an employee recognition fair.

FIGURE 42: SAMPLE PAYROLL STUFFER/FLYER

Announcing A New, Exciting Program: Spot Recognition

1. What is this program?
   It is a program that recognizes you immediately for your contributions.

2. Why do we need this program?
   Your contributions are important to Major Corporation and we want to recognize you for them.

3. What will I get out of the program?
   A number of items, ranging from gift certificates to paid time off, will be awarded to employees.

4. Who will be recognizing me?
   Your supervisor, a member of the administrative team and our customers.

5. When does the program begin?
   July 1, 2004

6. How can I learn more?
   • You will receive more information at general information sessions beginning June 1, 2004. Times and places of these sessions will be posted in your department and on our intranet site.
   • You will also receive a letter which provides details about the program within the next 7 days. PLEASE READ THIS LETTER and let us know what you think on our intranet site.

Some organizations may be so dispersed, or have locations with only a few employees, that a recognition fair may be impractical. In those cases, the best alternative to a fair would be to use theme-related media, such as in-house videos that generate fun and excitement about the program. Program training also can revolve around a fun theme (e.g., "You Are a Star!"). Theme-related training generates interest and enthusiasm.

The biggest caution is that theme-related events should be augmented with other communication approaches. These events generate short-term enthusiasm, but the message can soon be forgotten unless it is repeatedly reinforced.

Reviewing Implementation Strategies

A final review of all implementation strategies must be conducted before the program is communicated. The review has six basic steps:

Step 1 — Determine who needs to know in advance. Who are the key players in the implementation process? The answer to this question will drive how to roll out the program. Key players include the program coordinator, recognition committee, HR representatives, senior leaders, managers and program trainers. These individuals all play a major role in the implementation process, and must be prepared to discuss and champion the new program.

Step 2 — Review program themes and key messages. The purpose of this final review is to determine that program themes and messages accurately depict what the organization wants to accomplish.

Step 3 — Identify all communication channels. As stated, the grapevine is one channel that should not be overlooked. Informal leaders should be included in the implementation process so they can feed the grapevine with accurate information. Other channels include departmental meetings, organizational newsletters, unions (if applicable), intranet and Internet sites and the various media previously discussed.

Step 4 — Pilot the program with a select group or department. If possible, the program could be piloted or a dress rehearsal done with a small group of employees. This group can then identify any potential problems before the program is fully implemented.

Step 5 — Review and revise, as necessary, the communication plan. Based on data received during the pilot, the plan may need to be tweaked. A dress rehearsal with key players and select employees should provide some suggestions on what works well and what needs to be adjusted.

Step 6 — Make sure the timing of the program implementation does not conflict with any other major changes. The program's impact will be much less if it must compete with other major organizational initiatives.

After completing this final review and making any necessary adjustments, the program is ready to be implemented and communicated to employees.

FIGURE 43: ESSENTIAL ELEMENTS OF AN EMPLOYEE RECOGNITION FAIR		
Element	**Creative Examples**	**Justification**
Develop a theme for the event.	"Our Employees Are All-Stars" (A slide presentation or in-house video depicting employees at their work areas could be used.)	Builds interest and excitement about the event and the program
Structure the event around the program.	• If a booth arrangement is used, each booth should be some aspect of the program (e.g., awards, eligibility, types of recognition events, etc.). • Provide a passport to employees and have it stamped at each information booth or area.	Allows employees to relate the event to the program
Create a fun and exciting event.	• Provide an event that uses colorful posters, booths and eye-catching items, such as balloons and colored lights. • Use music if not too distracting. • Use tour guides (i.e., recognition committee) to take employees through the event.	Builds employee interest in the program
Effectively demonstrate the importance of the program.	• Provide basic facts and statistics about employee contributions. • Use testimonials to be displayed prominently during the fair.	Builds credibility and buy-in from employees
Provide printed resource materials.	• Distribute program brochures and summaries to employees at the fair.	Provides reference materials that can be used after attending the fair
Identify all available resources.	• Post pictures of the recognition committee and program coordinator. • Provide a resource checklist to employees as they enter the fair. • Have employees complete a short survey about program resources at the last information booth before exiting the fair.	Employees need to know who can answer their questions.
Provide fun events. Ensure organizational leaders are visible at the fair.	• Employees can play games, such as "Wheel of Recognition." Each game puzzle can be tied back to an aspect of the program. • Each booth at the fair could have some fun activity.	Employees enjoy learning in a fun atmosphere.

FIGURE 43: ESSENTIAL ELEMENTS OF AN EMPLOYEE RECOGNITION FAIR (CONTINUED)		
Elements	Creative Examples	Justification
Provide refreshments and food, if possible.	• Senior leaders and members of the recognition committee should attend and actively participate in the fair. • Provide theme-related food and drink (e.g., hot dogs, hamburgers and drinks, if it is a summer event).	The program will have greater credibility if employees see senior leaders support it. Attracts employees to the fair
Offer door prizes.	• Give attendees a small prize, such as a plastic drink mug with the program theme printed on it. • Have a grand prize drawing at the close of the fair. The grand prize could be a weekend retreat or a gift certificate. (Reminder: This may be a taxable item, depending on the cost.)	Provides a fun reminder of the program

8

Determining Legal Requirements and Tax Liability

There are a number of Internal Revenue Service (IRS) and federal regulations that govern recognition programs. The regulations governing recognition programs focus on eight key criteria:

1. **Cash versus non-cash**. Programs granting a direct cash award are always subject to direct taxation. Non-cash programs that offer a significant tangible value may be subject to taxation and other restrictions.

2. **Nominal value of the award.** The IRS determines the definition of nominal value. Currently, this definition is unclear and unresolved by the IRS. Proposed guidelines [i.e., Section 274-8(c)(5)(ii)] state that $50 is nominal value for tax purposes. To be eligible for exclusion at all, the award must be given under the guidelines established by a written plan or program in any given year. If an award is defined as nominal, it can be excluded from the total award costs used to determine the average cost per recipient. The average cost per recipient determines the tax liability of the plan and cannot exceed established IRS limits.

3. **Qualified versus nonqualified.** According to the Internal Revenue Code, a qualified plan is an established written plan or program that does not discriminate in favor of highly compensated employees (Note: This is currently set at an annual income of $85,000 or more). An employee recognition program will not be treated as a qualified plan for any taxable year if the average cost of all employee award programs provided by the employer during the year exceeds $400 per recipient. According to IRS regulations, average cost shall be determined by including the entire cost of qualified plan awards, without taking into account employee achievement awards of nominal value. The deduction limitation is increased to $1,600 per employee, as long as the employee recognition award is made under the following guidelines:

   A) The award given to the employee must be an employer transfer item of "tangible personal property" for safety achievement or length of service. Impact: Traditional service awards and safety recognition programs have a favorable tax treatment under IRS guidelines.

   B) The award must be given as part of a meaningful presentation. Impact: The traditional service awards banquet or safety recognition retreat still meets the intent of IRS guidelines.

   C) The award cannot be disguised compensation to the employee.

Impact: The award will not qualify for favorable tax treatment if it is used in lieu of awarding cash bonuses or given in conjunction with the annual performance evaluation.

D) The requirement that an award must be an item of "tangible personal property" must be carefully scrutinized. The IRS does not specifically define this term, but does provide some guidelines regarding its interpretation. For example, the award cannot be in cash or a gift certificate that can readily be converted into cash. Impact: Any gift certificate that can be easily converted into cash does not represent "tangible personal property" and will not be given favorable tax treatment.

A service award granted at five-year increments generally can be excluded unless the employee has received another length of service award of significant value. Safety awards to full-time employees also are generally excluded from taxable income unless, during the taxable year, all other employee awards for safety achievement exceed 10 percent of the eligible employee population. If the awards do exceed 10 percent of the eligible full-time employees, any additional safety awards are not tax deductible.

4. **Written versus nonwritten plans.** Written plans have more favorable tax treatment and meet the criteria established for qualified award plans. Nonwritten plans generally are not given favorable tax treatment unless the value of the award has a "de minimis" benefit value.

5. **De minimis benefit.** Under IRS regulations, any award with such a small value, after taking into account similar benefits provided to employees, that accounting for the benefit would be impracticable, is excluded from the employee's gross income. Impact: Many of the relatively inexpensive items used in an informal recognition program would be excluded from the employee's gross income. The frequency of providing awards with de minimis value also should be monitored. If the accumulated value of the awards becomes comparable to other benefits programs, the favorable tax treatment may no longer be in effect.

6. **Intangible value or benefit.** Recognition programs that focus on items such as open praise and employee motivation are obviously not subject to legal and tax restrictions. These programs provide employers the ability to recognize employees without creating administrative and legal frameworks. Personalized recognition from the supervisor still remains one of the best

ways to motivate employees. It should be an integral part of the total recognition effort.

7. **Specific exclusions.** Some recognition and benefits programs are not subject to employment taxes as defined in the Internal Revenue Code. In addition to the de minimis benefits discussed, the following programs are specifically identified as excluded from taxation:

- *No-additional-cost service* — This is a service offered for sale to customers in which the employee works at no substantial additional cost, including lost revenue, to the employer. Examples include airline, bus and train tickets, and telephone services provided free or at reduced rates by an employer in the line of business in which the employee works. Impact: Depending on the products and services provided to the employee by the employer, a favorable tax treatment could be obtained by using the employer's own services or products as a recognition award. However, the services or products cannot be transferred to a nonemployee in exchange for cash. Any direct cash incentive would lose the favorable tax advantage.

- *Qualified employee discount* — This is a discount that, if offered for property, is not more than the employer's gross profit percentage. If offered for services, the discount is not more than 20 percent of the price for services offered to customers. Impact: Recognition programs that offer employee discounts must adhere to these provisions or have the discount included as taxable income to the employee.

- *Working condition fringe benefit* — This is any property or service provided to an employee that could be deducted as a business expense if the employee had paid for it. Examples include a company car for business use and subscriptions to business magazines. Limitation: There must be substantial restrictions on personal use of the property by the employee in order to qualify as a tax-exempt benefit. Impact: It is important to carefully structure these benefits in order to meet tax guidelines. For example, a company car must truly be restricted to business use to qualify.

- *Qualified transportation fringe benefit* — This includes transit passes, transportation in a commuter highway vehicle to and from work and qualified parking at or near the place of work. Monetary limits: The combined exclusion for transit passes and transportation cannot exceed $65 per month (as of 2001); the exclusion for parking cannot exceed $180 per month (2001). Limitation: Employees may be given a choice of any qualified transportation fringe benefit or cash compensation without losing the exclusion of the qualified transportation fringe benefit from income and employment taxes. However, the cash is considered part of the worker's income and subject to employment taxes. Impact: The exclusions directly impact the amount of benefit provided to employees. The exclusion does not apply to partners, 2 percent or more shareholders in an S corporation or independent contractors. It has been common practice to give "free parking spaces" as recognition. This practice needs to be scrutinized in light of these provisions.

- *Qualified tuition reduction* — This is a reduction for tuition that an educational organization provides to its employees for courses generally below the graduate level.

8. **On premises versus off site.** An on-premises gym or other athletic facility would be excluded from the employee's income. This must be a facility provided and operated by the employer if substantially all the use is by employees, their spouses and dependent children. The athletic facility must be located on premises the company owns or leases. It does not have to be located on the employer's business premises. This exclusion does not apply to an athletic facility for residential use (i.e., a facility that is part of a resort). The major impact is that the employer can provide fitness services to its employees and dependents in a favorable tax arrangement. Another on-premises recognition program that is not directly covered by tax codes is an on-site educational program. If this program is for the employee's continuing education or training purposes, the program is tax-exempt. Providing lodging to an employee on business premises also can be excluded from that individual's gross income if it meets the following conditions:

A) It is furnished on the employer's business premises.

B) It is furnished for the employer's convenience. An example would be an ambulance worker who is provided free lodging to be able to respond to emergencies.

C) The employee must accept it as a condition of employment. For example, the ambulance worker probably will be requested to be on business premises as a condition of employment.

Figure 44 (Page 119) provides a checklist for determining tax liability. This checklist can be used as a quick reference guide only. The actual regulations should be verified with the applicable tax codes governing the benefits/recognition program. This tax liability discussion is subject to change as new regulations and proposed guidelines become part of the tax codes.

Legal Compliance

The biggest compliance challenge in developing recognition programs is that many plan designs closely resemble existing employee benefits plans. For example, tying recognition to specific payout formulas could result in additional legal compliance problems. While there certainly is nothing wrong with granting cash recognition or tying it to a payout formula, the cash is not only subject to taxation but also to certain pay laws such as the Fair Labor Standards Act (FLSA).

According to the FLSA, any nondiscretionary bonus paid to nonexempt employees must be included in calculating the regular rate for determining overtime compensation. A nondiscretionary bonus is an incentive or bonus paid out based on predetermined formulas, established criteria or a stated performance goal.

Discretionary bonuses are not based on predetermined criteria or prior agreement. Such bonuses represent payments made at the sole discretion of the employer. While such bonuses are taxable, a discretionary bonus is not included in overtime calculations. Other legislation such as the Equal Pay Act and the civil rights acts also must be closely scrutinized to avoid charges of gender bias or favoritism in granting the recognition. The following types of bonuses must be included in FLSA overtime pay calculations:

- Attendance bonuses
- Production bonuses, both individual and group
- Bonuses for quality and accuracy of work
- Length-of-service bonuses
- Bonuses promised to employees at the time of hiring
- Bonuses provided for in union contracts.

The following bonuses can be ignored when computing overtime pay under the FLSA:

- Christmas bonuses
- Gift bonuses
- Bonuses wholly within the employer's discretion

FIGURE 44: CHECKLIST FOR DETERMINING TAX LIABILITY			
Type of Benefit/Recognition Program	Federal Income Tax Withholding	Social Security and Medicare	Federal Unemployment
Achievement Awards	Exempt 1 up to certain limit	Exempt 1 up to certain limit	Exempt 1 up to certain limit
Cash Bonus Plan	Taxable	Taxable	Taxable
D eminimis (Minimal) Benefits	Exempt	Exempt	Exempt
Employee Discounts	Exempt 1 up to certain limits.		
Gifts	Exempt up to $25 if not redeemable in cash		
Intangible Programs providing motivational feedback to employees (i.e. Thank you(s), congratulatory citations)	Exempt	Exempt	Exempt
No-additional-cost services	Exempt 2	Exempt 2	Exempt 2
Qualified Recognition/ Benefits Programs	Must meet certain criteria to be exempt (see discussion in text)		
Safety Programs/Service Awards Programs	Can be exempt if they meet certain criteria — see discussion on qualified versus nonqualified plans in the text.		
Work Condition Benefits	Exempt	Exempt	Exempt

Notes:
1. Exemption does not apply to S corporation employees who are 2% shareholders.
2. Exemption does not apply to certain highly compensated employees.

- Profit-sharing bonuses paid pursuant to profit-sharing plans and trusts.

In addition to compensation-based plans, some programs tie in recognition with certain existing benefits programs. Some notable examples include additional contributions to the employee's 401(k) plan, dependent care assistance and supplemental health or investment programs that are offered to a select few as recognition. Laws governing employee benefits programs should be reviewed to determine the additional compliance issues created by these creative approaches. Employers should review the following benefits and tax laws before implementing these recognition approaches:

- **The Employee Retirement Income Security Act of 1974 (ERISA)** — Governs 401(k) retirement plans and other pension approaches. Caution: Contributing lump sums to the 401(k) plan as recognition could cause problems when the required discrimination testing is done for the retirement program.
- **Internal Revenue Code (Section 125)** — Governs cafeteria benefits programs and flexible spending accounts. In the example, the cash received in the cafeteria plan is obviously taxable. Dependent care assistance also may be impacted by this tax code.
- **The Tax Reform Acts and Budget Reconciliation Acts** — Established criteria for providing employee benefit tax incentives that are limited to those benefits that do not discriminate in favor of the highly compensated employee. In the example, providing investment incentives as recognition to a select few may violate the spirit of this law.
- **The Consolidated Omnibus Budget Reconciliation Act (COBRA)** — Federal legislation that governs extending health-care coverage in the event the employee is terminated, divorced, suffers a loss of work hours or dies. If additional health-care coverage is offered as an incentive, it may be impacted by this legislation.

These laws and regulations represent the most common legal compliance legislation that employers need to closely review. Obviously, there are many other laws, regulations and tax codes to consider when implementing a new program. However, employers that follow some simple rules when communicating the program to employees can satisfy many of the regulatory requirements. Figure 45 (Page 123) details these rules.

It is important to design written communications that meet the intent of the law, but also can be easily understood by all participants. Written communications can use a question and answer approach. For example, consider the second rule with regard to program exclusions:

Question: What performance areas are not included in the recognition program?

Answer: If the employee performs a duty or provides a service for a customer that is not beyond the normal expectations for his/her position, he/she will not be eligible for additional recognition. An example would be directing the customer to the appropriate area of the organization to receive service.

Caution: It is important to carefully review all written communication before sending it to employees. Once the program is put in writing or a policy format, employees can use it against the organization should a legal challenge occur.

The organization can increase its ability to successfully defend employee challenges by implementing two program elements:

1. **Implementing and communicating a problem-solving procedure.** This may seem like overkill, but employees will complain if they perceive inequities in program administration. The problem-solving procedure serves as a "grievance process" that can be used by the employee to voice concerns. The process should be simple and easy to use. It should include the following:

   - Who will hear the employee grievance (e.g., program coordinator, recognition committee or executive staff member)?
   - How does the employee access the process? It could be as easy as talking to the program coordinator or a recognition committee member.
   - How long will it take for the employee to receive an answer? This should be a relatively short time frame for the employee. In most cases, it should not exceed five working days.

2. **Establishing a sunset provision, if appropriate.** A sunset provision establishes under what conditions the program will be continued or terminated. A formal recognition program that is built around cash or awards with significant tangible value should be reviewed at least annually. Informal programs that have de minimis or intangible awards generally do not need a sunset provision. These programs can be discontinued at any time. The following basic sunset provision could be used:

Major Corporation will review this program at least annually to determine if it still meets the needs of the organization and its employees. Based on this review, Major Corporation reserves the right to discontinue, change or revise the recognition program at its discretion.

These preventive elements will help the organization meet the legal intent of the laws and regulations discussed. Regulatory agencies focus on how willing the organization is to resolve employee concerns and communicate program requirements. Legal and tax requirements should not be a deterrent to implementing a recognition program. Most recognition approaches require generally few regulations. The organization should be more concerned about successfully communicating the program. If it is successfully communicated, then employees and supervisors will see the program as an important tool in the workplace.

FIGURE 45: RULES FOR DEVELOPING WRITTEN COMMUNICATIONS THAT COMPLY WITH REGULATORY GUIDELINES	
Guiding Rule	**Key Component(s)**
Develop written criteria.	• Who is eligible • Program's purpose • Brief definition of the program
Identify program exclusions.	• What performance or behavior is excluded from recognition? • Identify expected performance standards, if appropriate.
Determine monetary limits for the program.	• Identify de minimis awards.
Participate in developing the program theme.	• Establish dollar limits for cash and non-cash awards. • Clearly identify formula-based limits.
Clearly spell out the procedure for taxing awards.	• Identify under what conditions the award will be taxed, if appropriate.
Identify areas of legal compliance (if appropriate).	• FLSA overtime requirements • Regulatory reporting requirements, if appropriate • Federal, state and local regulations, if appropriate
Identify the types of awards.	• Cash awards • Non-cash awards • Tangible recognition items • Intangible recognition • Formal and informal programs • Planned and unplanned recognition approaches
Develop procedures for conducting recognition.	• How employee can be recognized • Who can recommend the employee for recognition (e.g., co-workers, supervisors, vendors, customers, etc.) • Documenting the recognition event • Award ceremonies and other formal presentation events, if appropriate • Procedure for records retention related to the program

FIGURE 45: RULES FOR DEVELOPING WRITTEN COMMUNICATIONS THAT COMPLY WITH REGULATORY GUIDELINES (CONTINUED)	
Guiding Rule	**Key Component(s)**
Identify responsible parties.	• Person(s) responsible for overall program administration • Person(s) responsible for conducting the recognition event • Person(s) responsible for review and approval of the program • Person(s) responsible for resolving program complaints and concerns
Establish a sunset provision (if appropriate).	• Program review process • Frequency of program review • Conditions under which the program can be terminated or continued

9

Evaluating Program Effectiveness

After the program is implemented, the final step is to evaluate its effectiveness. The evaluation process is continuous and has two goals:

- To determine if the program is meeting its objectives
- To identify program successes and communicate them to key stakeholders.

These goals should be pursued with the same vigor as monitoring a new incentive plan or managed care program. A big reason that recognition programs are not taken seriously is organizations often fail to adequately monitor their success. Recognition will fail in the long run if leaders are not accountable for its effectiveness. Like fiscal measures, some key indicators must be measured and successes communicated.

This chapter will review a number of tools for measuring the program's effectiveness. It also is essential that leaders monitor their own commitment to the recognition process. The Recognition Log (See Appendix) provides a system for the leader to monitor daily program usage. This measurement tool may appear to be simplistic, but it helps keep recognition at a "top of the mind awareness" for the leader. The log asks the leader to do the following:

- Describe the action or the event being recognized.
- Identify who observed the action or event.
- Describe what makes the action exceptional.

The following questions should be answered:

- What standards were used, if any?
- When did the action or event occur?
- What type of recognition was given to the employee?

The log also indicates to the leader that recognition is important to the organization. The log is the leader's personal measurement tool. Let's look at some of the tools the organization can use to measure overall program effectiveness.

The Employee Recognition Scorecard

The Employee Recognition Scorecard is the definitive tool for communicating the program's effectiveness. The scorecard details the program performance by key indicators. In Chapter 2 (see Figure 13), these indicators were identified. They should be helpful in building the scorecard. Figure 46 (Page 129) provides a sample scorecard that has six basic areas, including most of the previously discussed key indicators:

- **General program measures** — These include an accounting of the total number of employees recognized for the quarter. It also includes a quarterly approval rating of the program by key stakeholders. A quarterly survey of at least a randomly selected number of employees and participants is highly recommended. The example also includes a summary of the Star Card program that was implemented to reward employees for excellent customer service. There is a later tie-in with the customer service area, which exceeded expectations and would in fact probably place the organization in a very enviable position.
- **Program cost** — This includes total program cost for the quarter, cost per full-time employee and program cost as a percent of payroll.
- **Quality** — Three areas can be measured, including safety suggestions (if the safety program is a component of the recognition program), work process improvements and recognition events that can be directly tied to productivity improvements and service delivery. Some organizations may want to exclude this area of the scorecard, particularly if a Total Quality Improvement program already measures the components.
- **Customer service** — If the organization does a customer satisfaction survey, and it can be tied back to recognition (e.g., Star Card program), the results should be monitored. In the example, the Star Card program has dramatically impacted customer service. Customer satisfaction levels exceeded the target of an 85 percent satisfaction level by 7 percent. The organization awarded 490 Star Cards to employees for excellent customer service during the first quarter. This is an excellent example of how employee recognition ties in to the organization's success.
- **Employee morale** — This includes the results of any quarterly or annual employee surveys on job satisfaction levels. The current morale level should be compared to the morale index before the recognition program is implemented. The survey should ask employees: "How has the employee recognition program affected your personal morale?"
- **Employee retention** — The three measures in the example include organizational turnover, job vacancy rate and turnaround time to fill a vacant position. Other possible measures include number of job transfers, promotions and feedback about employee recognition on exit interviews.

These six areas can be included in the scorecard, but other organizations may have fewer or more areas to be measured. The program coordinator is responsible for designing and maintaining the scorecard with input from the recognition committee. The scorecard should be presented to the board of directors, the chief executive officer, senior leadership and other key stakeholders at least quarterly to show the value of the employee recognition program. Some results (e.g., customer service and employee retention) should be shared with supervisors, customers and employees.

The scorecard communicates to key stakeholders that employee recognition is an integral part of the organization's culture. It also provides an easy method for monitoring the areas of recognition that are doing well and the areas that need improving. It is obvious from the example that employee recognition is doing quite well in the first quarter of the year. Actual results have exceeded target levels in all areas except program cost. Since this is a new program, it is common for costs to exceed target levels during initial implementation. However, costs must still be monitored closely to prevent recognition from being a program that "hands out cash and other free things without leaders being accountable for the ultimate budgetary consequences." Reminder: Program cost overruns or inadequate recognition budgets can kill the program because too much or not enough money is being spent on employee recognition. The scorecard cannot be completed without data from various other measurement sources (e.g., surveys, audits, customer surveys and HR statistics). The program coordinator must assemble this data to complete the scorecard and assure the following:

- The scorecard data is accurate and complete.
- Leaders and other key stakeholders are trained on how to read and use the scorecard.
- The scorecard does not overstate or understate program results.
- The scorecard is communicated on a consistent and timely basis.

If these guidelines are followed, the scorecard will be seen as credible and objective.

Measurement Tools

Three essential measurement tools — recognition survey, leadership assessment and program audit — supplement the scorecard. These tools are easy to use and provide data for the scorecard.

Quarter/Month: Test Quarter, XXXX

GENERAL PROGRAM MEASURES

MEASURE	TARGET	ACTUAL	VARIANCE	YTD VARIANCE
1. Number of Star Cards given to employees	450 per quarter	490	+40	+40
2. Spot recognition awards granted	250	283	+33	+33
3. Total number of employees recognized	600	625	+25	+25
4. Quarterly approval rating of the program by employees	85%	92%	+7%	+7%

PROGRAM COST

COST MEASURE	TARGET	ACTUAL	VARIANCE	YTD VARIANCE
1. Total quarterly cost	$150,000	$160,000	+$10,000	+$10,000
2. Cost per full-time equivalent employee (3,000 FTEs)	$50	$53.33	+$3.33 per FTE	+$3.33 per FTE
3. Recognition cost as a percent of payroll ($60,000,000)	1%	1.1%	+.1%	+.1%

QUALITY

QUALITY MEASURE	TARGET	ACTUAL	VARIANCE	YTD VARIANCE
1. Safety suggestions	25	22	(3)	(3)
2. Work process improvements	50	56	+6	+6
3. Recognized employees for performance tied to improving productivity or service delivery	25	27	+2	+2

CUSTOMER SERVICE

SERVICE MEASURE	TARGET	ACTUAL	VARIANCE	YTD VARIANCE
1. Percent of favorable response on customer survey	85%	92%	+7%	+7%
2. Customer compliments received	20	41	+21	+21

FIGURE 46: SAMPLE EMPLOYEE RECOGNITION SCORECARD (CONTINUED)				
EMPLOYEE MORALE				
MORALE INDICATOR	TARGET	ACTUAL	VARIANCE	YTD VARIANCE
1. Job satisfaction rating on quarterly department surveys	80%	88%	+8%	+8%
2. Morale index, which is a composite of annual job satisfaction scores and quarterly survey results, by department	75%	82%	+7%	+7%
EMPLOYEE RETENTION				
RETENTION MEASURE	TARGET	ACTUAL	VARIANCE	YTD VARIANCE
1. Organizational turnover rate	3.5% per quarter, 14% annually	2% for the quarter	(1.5%)	(1.5%)
2. Job vacancy rate	10%	6%	(4%)	(4%)
3. Turnaround time to fill a vacant position	21 days	16 days	(5 days)	(5 days)

Recognition Survey

The purpose of the recognition survey is to determine the program's employee approval rating. It should be conducted quarterly and limited to no more than five questions. Figure 47 (Page 132) provides a sample recognition survey. The survey can be used as a payroll stuffer, on the organization's intranet/Internet sites or in a direct mailing to the individual.

The 92% service rating on the sample scorecard equates to a 4.6 numeric rating compared to the target numeric rating of 4.25 (i.e., 85% approval rating). Five areas of satisfaction are covered by the sample survey:

1. **Individual** — Is the employee satisfied with the program?
2. **Intrinsic** — Does the program satisfy the employee's internal or personal needs?
3. **Extrinsic** — Does the program reward the employee appropriately?
4. **Program** — Is the program administered consistently?
5. **Employee** — Do other employees value the program?

The program coordinator can use the data from the survey to drill down on each area of satisfaction and make changes as needed.

Leadership Assessment

After the program has been implemented, leadership should be assessed on a quarterly basis to determine commitment to the program and skill level in administering it. This assessment provides valuable data to the organization about the leader's comfort level with the recognition efforts. Like the recognition survey, the leadership assessment should be brief and address five basic areas:

- The leader's comfort level with the program
- How much the leader values recognition as a management tool
- How well the leader feels trained on the program
- The leader's belief that the employee sees the program as important
- How committed the leader believes the organization is to recognition.

A sample leadership assessment is shown in Figure 48 (Page 134).

The program coordinator should report the results of the leadership assessment to the recognition committee and the senior leadership team. The last question is open-ended, and all comments should be summarized to protect the leader's anonymity. The assessment should be revised after the first year and include questions about long-term results. The program coordinator and the recognition committee also should share assessment results with the general management team. In fact, these quarterly updates also should include a summary of the recognition survey conducted with employees. At these updates, leaders should be encouraged to openly discuss their thoughts on program successes and areas for improvement.

Program Audit

The program coordinator and recognition committee should audit the program at least annually. The audit's purpose is to ensure the plan is being administered appropriately. The audit should review the following areas:

- Policies and procedures for the program to determine if they are being used appropriately
- Internal structure including the role of the recognition committee, program coordinator, senior leadership and others in administering the program (Note: This includes a total review of the infrastructure to determine if it needs to be changed. Senior leadership and the recognition committee will need to evaluate the program coordinator's effectiveness.)

Instructions: Please rate the effectiveness of the employee recognition program provided by Major Corporation by answering this brief questionnaire. For each of the following statements, indicate your agreement based on the following scale:

1 = Strongly Disagree
2 = Disagree
3 = Neutral-Neither Agree Nor Disagree
4 = Agree
5 = Strongly Disagree

1. I am satisfied with the employee recognition program offered by the organization.

      1   2   3   4   5

2. The recognition program makes me feel worthwhile and important to the organization.

      1   2   3   4   5

3. The rewards provided by the recognition program are meaningful and acceptable to me.

      1   2   3   4   5

4. The recognition program is administered consistently and fairly.

      1   2   3   4   5

5. I believe the recognition program is well understood and valued by employees.

      1   2   3   4   5

The approval rating would be derived from the above questionnaire by converting the rating scale as follows:

      1 = 20% approval rating
      2 = 40% approval rating
      3 = 60% approval rating
      4 = 80% approval rating
      5 =100% approval rating

- External resources and consultants to ensure the services provided met organizational and contractual standards
- Tax and legal requirements — these must be met and immediate adjustments made if the program fails to comply with regulatory guidelines
- Training of leaders to ensure appropriate information and guidance are provided
- Program costs to make sure the program is within budgetary guidelines
- Usage patterns to determine what work areas are effectively using the program and the areas not using the program
- Program goals and objectives to determine if the program is meeting the organization's needs
- Feedback received from all key stakeholders (e.g., employee survey, leadership assessment, employee opinion survey, management and board meetings).

The audit could take up to two weeks to complete, and the program coordinator will need assistance and cooperation from employees, managers, vendors and senior leaders. Audit results should be reported to the CEO, senior leaders, managers and employees. The recognition committee should be actively involved in every step of the audit process. Audit results should be benchmarked, if possible, with similar organizations. Benchmarking is yet another checkpoint to determine how the program is doing. A few sample audit questions follow:

Do the policies and procedures support the program objectives?

     ___YES   ___NO

Have all leaders received training on employee recognition?

     ___YES   ___NO

Are contracts with vendors and consultants monitored for consistency and accuracy?

     ___YES   ___NO

Are program costs within established budget limits?

     ___YES   ___NO

Do payroll practices support the legal and tax requirements when recognition is granted?

     ___YES   ___NO

Instructions: Please help us determine the effectiveness of the organization's employee recognition program. For each of the following statements, indicate your level of agreement based on the scale below:

1 = Strongly Disagree
2 = Disagree
3 = Neutral-Neither Agree Nor Disagree
4 = Agree
5 = Strongly Disagree

1. I am comfortable using the recognition program to reward employees.

     1 2 3 4 5

2. I believe the recognition program has given me an additional tool to motivate employees.

     1 2 3 4 5

3. I have been appropriately trained on how to effectively use the employee recognition program.

     1 2 3 4 5

4. Employees believe the recognition program is an important part of their work experience.

     1 2 3 4 5

5. The organization is committed to recognizing and rewarding employees.

     1 2 3 4 5

6. Do you have any suggestions regarding employee recognition:

_____
_____
_____
_____
_____

What areas have used the program with consistency?

_____

_____

_____

_____

What areas have not used the program consistently?

_____

_____

_____

The audit will include more than asking questions of key stakeholders. It should incorporate a review of all available scorecards, payroll practices, the recognition budget, consultant and vendor contracts, training logs, survey data and usage statistics. Some organizations may want to use an outside source to conduct the audit. Using an outside source is especially helpful when auditing the program for the first time. If one source is used, the program coordinator and recognition committee should be kept informed of the audit progress and be actively involved, if possible.

Assessing Program Objectives

As part of the evaluation process, an assessment will determine if the program has met its goals and objectives. An assessment of program objectives against the sample scorecard should include the following elements:

- Defined program objectives
- Measurement criteria (the data and approaches used to assess)
- Rating criteria (e.g., exceeds expectations, meets expectations, does not meet expectations)
- Justifications (i.e., how the rating was derived)
- Assigned responsibility (i.e., the party responsible for assessing the objective on an ongoing basis).

The measurement criteria include the methods used to assess the objective. These methods include direct observation by the organization, program usage, data sources such as surveys and program audits. The rating scale should tie back to the program's scorecard. For example, if a program aspect meets the target on the scorecard, it generally will mean the objective meets expectations. The only exception to this rule is when direct observation by the leader or program coordinator indicates the data is not telling the entire story. For example, when an organization has just given a significant market salary adjustment for a particular job category, it would be presumptuous to assume that employee recognition drastically impacted turnover for that job category.

Justification for the rating should be data driven if possible. For example, program utilization exceeded the goal by 20 percent based on the number of recognition events conducted during the first quarter. Finally, ongoing assessment should be assigned to an individual or committee (i.e., recognition committee) to ensure objectives are appropriately assessed. Figure 49 (Page 138) details an assessment of the program using these five elements.

The assessment indicates that the program exceeded expectations on three of the four objectives. This is an excellent start and should be communicated throughout the organization.

Communicating Program Success

Once the program has been implemented and evaluated, its success must be communicated at least quarterly to all key stakeholders. As the program matures, communication becomes the most important element for keeping recognition on an equal level with other total rewards programs.

The program must be continually communicated or participants will lose interest. Its goals and objectives must be widely understood and familiar to all participants. The goals should be discussed in departmental meetings and posted on organizational bulletin boards and Web sites. In addition to being communicated continuously, ongoing management depends on the following to be successful:

- *A visible program coordinator and recognition committee.* These individuals need to be the program champions. They must keep the program fresh and update it as better approaches and techniques are identified.
- *A continuous review and evaluation of program results.* The major point for ongoing management is to evaluate how the program is doing. This evaluation should identify if the program needs to be changed, left alone or ended.

- *The employee attraction and retention strategy.* Recognition must be more than a "feel good" program. Effective programs are embraced as a vital part of the employment experience.
- *The orientation program for new employees.* As employees come into the organization, recognition must be communicated as important to their work life. Too often, it is given very little time in the orientation process. As a result, recognition's impact is lost as employees enter the organization.
- *The organization's culture.* The best ways for recognition to become part of the culture is to keep reinforcing its importance. Examples of excellent customer service and employee performance need to be communicated continuously. Recognition should be discussed at every departmental meeting. Program results should be communicated at least quarterly to senior leaders and board members, if possible. The more recognition is talked about and communicated, the easier it will be for all key stakeholders to see it as part of the organization's culture. It is seen as "the way we do business."

Finally, the organization must pay attention to program cost and return on investment. The program should be reviewed quarterly to determine if the cost outlays are worth the benefits received. This is not a simple process because some benefits have an intrinsic value. A good recognition program helps the organization build a positive working environment. In turn, this saves the company attraction and retention costs, improves productivity and in short makes for a happier place to work.

Quarterly Program Summary

The scorecard and the program assessment are two excellent tools for communicating with key stakeholders. Other methods have been discussed including an annual theme-related event dedicated to recognition, ongoing training with leaders about how to effectively recognize employees and frequent feedback sessions with employees and leaders. The final tool for communicating success is the quarterly program summary. The summary should be a one-page highlight of successes during that quarter. Rather than act as a newsletter, it functions as a program update. The summary can be sent to key stakeholders, placed on the organization's Internet/intranet sites and distributed during feedback sessions with employees and leaders. It should be provided to board members, the CEO, senior leaders, employees and managers, and should be made available to customers. Figure 50 (Page 140) provides a sample program summary. The sample is brief and probably could be expanded to include more updates if available.

The summary can be customized depending on the work group. The in-house marketing department, if available, can assist in preparing the summary. It not only should provide program statistics, but also generate excitement about the program.

FIGURE 49: SAMPLE PROGRAM ASSESSMENT				
Program Objective Responsibility	Measurement Criteria	Rating Criteria	Justification	Assigned
To provide a program to reward employees who exceeded expected performance levels by at least 10%	Performance data Scorecard data	Exceeds expectations	Recognized 27 employees for exceeding productivity levels compared to target level of 25 employees during the first quarter	Department manager Program coordinator
To recognize employees who have made meaningful contributions to customer service	Survey data Star Card usage Direct observation	Exceeds expectations	Recognized 490 employees for excellent customer service during the first quarter compared to the target of 450	Program coordinator Recognition committee
Achieve at least a 10% improvement in job satisfaction	Employee surveys Scorecard data	Met expectations	Quarterly job satisfaction was 88% compared to target of 80%	Program coordinator
Reduce employee turnover by 20%	Turnover data Scorecard data	Exceeds expectations	Quarterly turnover was 2%, which was 43% less than expected level of 3.5%	Program coordinator Senior leadership

Summary

This publication has provided a step-by-step guide on how to construct an employee recognition program that will be fundamentally sound and easy to implement. It still is up to the organization to integrate recognition into the total rewards program. This is no small task but can be accomplished if there is complete commitment from all key stakeholders. There are five ways to increase the likelihood of the program's success:

- Solicit input from all stakeholders about the program on a regular and consistent basis.
- Commit enough financial resources to the program to make it meaningful to employees. Successful programs require a minimum funding level of 1 percent to 2 percent of the payroll.
- Make sure senior leadership is committed to the program before implementing it. If senior leadership is excited about the program, chances are it will be successful.
- Train leaders how to effectively recognize employees. This will increase the comfort level of the leader about employee recognition. Training should be ongoing at least annually.
- Communicate, communicate and communicate. No program will be successful if it is not communicated continuously. This keeps the program fresh and exciting. It also gives it "top of the mind awareness" with all key stakeholders.

Remember, what makes organizations truly unique is their reputation for valuing and recognizing their employees. Employee recognition can help your company become an exciting place for employees to work.

	FIGURE 50: QUARTERLY PROGRAM SUMMARY

Jan. 1 - March 31, XXXX

Star Card Program:	There were 490 employees recognized for giving excellent customer service during the first quarter. We had a record 41 customer compliments during the quarter, as well. If you know an employee who gives excellent customer service, call the Human Resources Department at Extension XXXX or contact your supervisor.
Spot Recognition:	We had 283 employees recognized on the spot for their outstanding contributions to the organization. The spot recognition program immediately rewards employees with cash and merchandise for examples of positive behavior and excellent work performance.
Recognition Fair:	All employees will be treated to a special event that focuses on employee recognition. The recognition fair will be held on May 10-12 at all our locations. The fair will provide information about employee recognition in a fun event. Refreshments will be served and door prizes awarded. You just might see a co-worker on the big screen as the fair's theme is "All Our Employees Are Stars." Come join in the fun.
Service Awards:	The service awards banquet was held on March 10 and 11. We recognized 375 employees for their long-term service with a banquet and service award. We had 78 employees with more than 20 years of service. Congratulations to all our employees for their commitment to Major Corporation.
Program Summary:	We had 1,571 employees participate in our quarterly survey of the recognition program. Thanks to their input we learned that the program is providing value to our employees. The survey respondents rated the program at a 92% approval level. If you would like to participate in the next survey, please look on our intranet site at www.xxxx.xxxx, or surveys will be available in your department on June 5, XXXX. We also had 1,793 employees participate in departmental work surveys. 88% of the respondents liked their job and stated that employee recognition had added a great deal to the working environment. We will continue to do these short surveys quarterly. Your participation is greatly appreciated.

10

Case Studies

Major Corporation (A Fictional Example)

- Product/Service: Paint Products
- Number of Full-Time Equivalent Employees: 3,000
- Percent of Payroll Committed to Recognition: 1
- Headquarters: San Diego, Calif.
- Other Locations: Fresno, Calif.

In the past year, Major Corporation has developed some new approaches to employee recognition. Employee recognition had been a "hit or miss" proposition geared mostly to safety suggestions. The organization's turnover rate had exceeded 30 percent in the past two years compared to the industry average of about 17 percent. In a recent employee opinion survey, job satisfaction was rated at a humiliating 48 percent favorable level. Employees complained on the survey about not being valued by the organization. Senior leadership realized it was time to make some positive changes.

Based on survey comments and turnover figures, senior leadership decided to investigate implementing a new employee recognition program. Formal and informal leaders were asked to serve on a recognition committee charged with assessing and implementing a program. The committee selected an individual from inside the organization to develop and implement the plan. The individual was highly respected throughout the organization and had a broad background in developing human resources programs.

The new coordinator and the recognition committee began assessing the company's readiness to implement a new program. The assessment began with in-depth interviews with organizational leaders to determine their commitment to employee recognition. A survey specifically focused on recognition was conducted with employees. Based on the assessment and survey data, it was determined that the organization wanted and would support a recognition program.

Developing the Recognition Program

From all the available data, the following program objectives were used to develop a solid recognition program:

- Increase employee's job satisfaction by at least 15 percent in the next year.
- Reduce employee turnover rates by at least 10 percent in the next year.

- Link employee recognition with other total rewards programs and integrate it into the organization's culture.

Figure 51 (Page 144) summarizes the employee recognition programs offered by Major Corporation.

Communication Approaches

A comprehensive plan was developed to communicate the new program. Many innovative approaches also were used during and after the program's implementation. Communication focused on increasing awareness of and support for employee recognition. Major Corporation incorporated the following communication approaches:

- A comprehensive training program was provided to leaders to increase their comfort with and awareness level of employee recognition.
- The CEO sent letters to employee homes announcing the recognition initiative.
- Information sessions were offered to all employees on all shifts and at both organizational locations.
- A detailed program description was posted on the organization's Internet/intranet sites.
- A "recognition hotline" was created for employees to have questions answered and provide program feedback.
- A "recognition fair," attended by 2,700 employees at both locations, provided program information and created excitement.
- A wide array of media sources communicated the program to key stakeholders. A video was developed featuring employees from Major Corporation. Colorful brochures and informational flyers were provided to employees, managers and even interested customers.
- Recognition is featured monthly at department/team meetings, in employee publications and on the organization's Web site.
- The new employee orientation program has integrated recognition, which also is featured prominently in the organization's recruitment program.
- A "Wall of Fame" is used to display pictures of employees who received recognition during the current quarter.

FIGURE 51: SUMMARY OF RECOGNITION FOR MAJOR CORPORATION			
PROGRAM DESCRIPTION	**REWARD PROVIDED**	**PROGRAM PURPOSE**	**TYPE OF PROGRAM**
SERVICE AWARDS — provided at the completion of every 5 years of service with the organization	• Service lapel pin or selected merchandise • Service awards banquet held annually	• To reward long-term service	• Non-cash • Formal recognition program
STAR CARD — spot recognition for extraordinary customer service	• Star Card that identifies what has been accomplished is given to employees immediately • All cards submitted for a monthly prize drawing at each location	• To build solid customer service	• Non-cash • Formal recognition program
SPOT RECOGNITION — spontaneous recognition provided to employees	• De minimis merchandise such as pins or other items • Gift certificates • Congratulatory citation (i.e., written congratulations from the supervisor)	• To recognize employees immediately for their achievements	• Non-cash • Informal recognition program
SAFETY SUGGESTION — employees are recognized for submitting safety improvements	• Small cash bonus • Plaque and lapel pin • Written documentation of the suggestion • Award given to individual during an awards luncheon	• To increase employees' awareness of safety issues	• Cash and non-cash • Formal recognition program
QUALITY IMPROVEMENT AWARDS — employees who make work process improvements are recognized	• Cash awards based on a formula depending on cost savings • Letter of appreciation from the CEO • Picture in organizational newsletter	• To encourage employees to make significant quality improvements	• Cash • Non-cash • Formal recognition program
DISCRETIONARY TEAM RECOGNITION — supervisor rewards team for extraordinary achievements	• Team luncheon • Write-up in the organizational newsletter • Gift certificates • Thank-you card	• To recognize a team for its contribution to the organization	• Informal recognition program

Program Successes

The organization conducts employee surveys on a quarterly basis. Last quarter, job satisfaction was at an impressive 72 percent level. This was a gain of 24 percent since the program began. This exceeded the program objective of a 10 percent increase in job satisfaction. Turnover has reduced from 30 percent to 18 percent, now near the industry average. Employees have expressed their appreciation of the program on surveys, in department meetings and on organizational Web sites. The organization has just been featured in a major business publication for its commitment to employees. New approaches to recognition are continuing to be explored by the organization to keep the program fresh and exciting. Senior leadership is solidly behind recognition and views it as strategic to the organization's success.

The Vanguard Group

The Vanguard Group, headquartered in Valley Forge, Pa., traces its roots to the founding of its first mutual fund, Wellington Fund, in 1928. Today, with more than $580 billion in net assets, Vanguard is the nation's second-largest mutual fund firm and a leading provider of company-sponsored retirement plan services. Vanguard services 15 million individual and institutional shareholders and offers 109 funds to U.S. investors and 29 additional funds in international markets. The Vanguard Group has offices in Valley Forge; Scottsdale, Ariz.; Charlotte, N.C.; Melbourne, Australia; Brussels, Belgium; London; and Tokyo.

Number of Crew Members (Vanguard's term for employee): 11,000 worldwide.

Recognition programs are budgeted to provide an award for one out of every six nonofficer crew members, based on prior-year headcount. Vanguard has several highly visible recognition and rewards programs on three distinct levels — corporate, individual and departmental.

Corporate-Level Recognition

Vanguard celebrates corporate anniversaries and achievements as well as other milestones in a variety of ways. On May 1, 2000, the company celebrated its 25th anniversary with festivities at its U.S. and international offices. In building lobbies decked in balloons and other decorations, crew members were presented a commemorative sterling silver "Jefferson Cup" imprinted with the

Vanguard ship logo and the inscription "25 Years of Excellence: 1975-2000." Posters bearing the last name of every crew member were also given out — many of which now adorn offices and cubicles throughout the company. In addition to these mementos, crew members received a cash award ($25 for every one year of service, with a minimum of $50 and a maximum of $250), an extra personal day and casual dress days every Friday from Memorial Day to Labor Day.

Vanguard also celebrates the attainment of asset milestones. On June 30, 1999, for example, Vanguard passed $500 billion in assets. The crew was rewarded with an attractive glass paperweight, a free lunch at the company cafeteria, a casual dress day and additional vacation time. Typically, a free lunch voucher or casual day is awarded for every $20 billion increase in net assets.

Individual Recognition

Superior performance and service to Vanguard clients by individual crew members are recognized in several ways:

- **Vanguard Award for Excellence.** A quarterly award is presented to a select group of crew members who demonstrate particular excellence in the performance of their duties and who embody the Vanguard "spirit," which is characterized by exceptional service, professionalism, creativity, initiative and a sense of humor. Vanguard Award for Excellence winners receive a pin; two tickets to a show or sporting event of their choice; $165 in cash; and a $500 contribution to the charity of their choice. Award recipients are nominated by their fellow crew members. Approximately 30 awards are presented each year to deserving crew members.

- **Vanguard Service Award.** Vanguard recognizes the dedication of crew members who have served the company for periods of five, 10, 15 and 20 years under a service award program. Honorees choose from a variety of high-quality gifts — from jewelry to desk sets. Many items feature the Vanguard logo. The gift, accompanied by a congratulatory letter from Vanguard CEO John J. Brennan, is presented to the honoree by his or her supervisor during an informal ceremony attended by peers and colleagues. The names of service award recipients also are printed in the company newsletter.

- **Vanguard Spot Bonus Award.** Crew members who provide exemplary service or successfully complete a special project may earn a $165 spot bonus award. In 2000, some 1,390 crew members were "spotted" with aggregate awards equaling nearly $229,350.

- **Vanguard Perfect Attendance Award.** Crew members who attain perfect attendance during the calendar year are provided two additional vacation days the following year. More than 1,000 crew members achieved perfect attendance in 2000. Crew members also were eligible for a raffle in which 12 $500 travel vouchers and three $1,000 travel vouchers were awarded. A special luncheon, attended by Vanguard's senior leadership team, was held in May 2001 for crew members with perfect attendance records of five or more years.
- **Birthday Coupon.** Even birthdays are celebrated at Vanguard, with a free lunch coupon presented to the crew member, along with a card signed by his or her managing director and immediate supervisor.

Departmental Recognition

Many individual departments sponsor recognition programs for notable performance and service. Vanguard Information/Technology Division has a Peer Recognition Award presented to outstanding crew members who are universally recognized by their co-workers. Other departments present tickets to local sporting and cultural events to recognize a project's completion or service "above and beyond the call of duty." Many departments promote teamwork and boost morale by designing shirts and other attire that feature that department's logo or slogan.

International Paper

Products: World's largest paper and forest products company. Businesses include manufacturing of paper, packaging and forest products for end-uses like copy paper, juice and milk cartons, and building lumber.

Number of Employees: 113,000 employees worldwide

World Headquarters: Stamford, Conn.

Operational Headquarters: Memphis, Tenn.

Locations: 650 locations in 50 countries. International Paper is a global company that exports its products to more than 130 nations.

The following is a discussion of the employee recognition programs offered at the Hopkinsville plant.

Attendance Incentive

Perfect Attendance Award — Employees with perfect attendance receive the following:

- 1 year: $25 gift card
- 2 years: $35 gift card
- 3 years: $45 gift card
- 4 years: $55 gift card
- 5 years: $70 gift card
- 6 years: $85 gift card
- 7 years: $100 gift card
- 7 years plus: $100 gift card for each year of perfect attendance
    - A personalized bronze plaque with the employee's name inscribed on it. Plaques are displayed prominently in the plant.
    - A letter from the plant manager.

Contribution to Plant Performance

Employee Incentive

The plant has established the following annual goals:

- Absence of customer complaints
- On-time shipments
- Operating efficiency
- Earnings Before Interest and Taxes (EBIT)
- Return on Investment (ROI)

- Total Incident Rate (TIR)
- Scrap.

Each goal has incentive dollars assigned to it. If all goals are met for the calendar year, each employee receives $1,000 in mid-January of the next calendar year. The amount an individual receives also depends on how many months they work in that calendar year.

Annual Bonus Program — Salaried Employees

Salaried employees have similar goals as production and maintenance employees. Salaried employees also have individual goals incorporated into their bonus program. The salaried incentive is based on a set percentage of the employee's base pay.

Cost Reduction Incentives — Salaried employees who submit viable cost reduction projects receive a monetary incentive once each year. The incentive amount is based on the dollar amount of the cost reduction project that has been implemented.

Pay for Skill (pay incentives) — The plant has implemented a Pay-for-Skill System. Under this system each job is broken down into specific, measurable tasks. The tasks are combined into "skill blocks." Each employee has required skill blocks that must be mastered. Advanced skill blocks (i.e., beyond those required) are strictly voluntary and employee driven.

Safety Incentives

B-Safe Bingo Safety Contest — Every employee gets a Bingo Card. Bingo numbers are drawn each week and posted on bulletin boards. For each month that the plant records no Occupational and Safety Health Administration injuries, the pot is $350. This contest is used six months of the year to keep it fresh and exciting.

Safety Wheel of Fortune Contest — If the plant goes an entire month without an injury recorded, all employees are assigned a number for the contest. These numbers are placed on the wheel of fortune. The wheel is spun until 14 employees win; each receives a gift card. This contest is used for six months of the year.

Safety Recognition Events — The plant has periodic recognition events for passing a safety milestone (i.e., XXX hours with no injuries recorded or XX years with no lost-time injuries). These recognition events range from pizza to a sit-down dinner. Other non-cash items include T-shirts, jackets, first-aid kits, lunch kits, etc.

Service Recognition

Employees receive a service pin for the following years of service: five, 10, 20 and 30 years. The pin is presented to the employee on or near the service anniversary date. Employees also are recognized in the plant communication system and in the company news magazine.

Appendix

- Trends in Employee Recognition 2005
- 2003 Recognition Survey

Trends in Employee Recognition 2005

A Survey of Members of WorldatWork and the National Association for Employee Recognition

Introduction and Methodology

This report summarizes the results of a survey conducted jointly by WorldatWork and the National Association for Employee Recognition (NAER) in February 2005 to identify and track trends in employee recognition. A similar WorldatWork and NAER member survey was conducted in both September 2003 and October 2002, providing a baseline of information about recognition program types, strategies, measures, administration, communication and training.

In February 2005, an updated survey instrument was sent electronically to 2,708 WorldatWork members and 599 NAER members. A total of 614 responses were received, a response rate of 19 percent. With this sample size and response rate, at a 95-percent confidence interval, the margin of error (or confidence interval) is +/- 4 percent.

The demographic profile of the survey's respondents is similar to that of the WorldatWork membership as a whole. The typical WorldatWork member works at the managerial level or higher in the headquarters of a large company in North America. Ninety-five percent of the *Fortune* 1,000 companies have an employee who is a WorldatWork member.

Summary of Key Findings

The report is divided into five sections:

    I. Screening Questions
    II. Strategy, Goals and Measures of Recognition
    III. Structure and Types of Recognition Programs
    IV. Program Administration and Support
    V. Recognition Program Communication and Training

Highlights from each of the sections follow:

I. Screening Questions

- Recognition remains important to organizations; 92 percent of organizations say employee recognition is occurring more often today within their organization versus 12 months ago.

- Nearly half of all respondents (48 percent), regardless of whether they have employee recognition programs in place, are considering adding new recognition programs in the next 12 months.

II. Strategy, Goals and Measures of Recognition

- Sixty percent of organizations with an employee recognition program have a written program strategy.
- The established objectives/goals of recognition programs have not changed much since the 2003 survey: "Creating a positive work environment" remains the most common goal at 81 percent of organizations. Motivating high performance, reinforcing desired behavior and creating a culture of recognition continue to drive recognition programs.
- Seventy-six percent of respondents believe their recognition programs are meeting outlined objectives and goals.
- Employee satisfaction surveys (used by 45 percent) are still the most common way organizations gauge the success of recognition programs, but participation rates and the number of employee recognition nominations received also are increasingly used as measures.

III. Structure and Types of Recognition Programs

- Length of service programs continue to be the most common type of recognition program offered (89 percent of organizations), with 87 percent of those companies having offered the program for more than five years.
- Almost seven in 10 organizations (69 percent) report they have a specific budget for recognition programs.

IV. Program Administration and Support

- The human resources department has primary responsibility for recognition program administration in the majority of organizations (57 percent).
- Fifty-five percent of respondents believe that senior management views recognition programs as an investment, while 13 percent think management views it as an expense.

V. Recognition Program Communication and Training

- Only 23 percent of respondents say that a formal training program for recognition programs exists within their organizations. Among the organizations that do have formal training, 69 percent rely on in-person training sessions.

Detailed Survey Results

Section I. Screening Questions

The first four questions of the survey (reported in this section) were asked of all respondents, regardless of whether they indicated their organization has an employee recognition program. The 11 percent who said they do not currently have a recognition program in response to question 1 (Figure 1) were asked to skip from question 4 to the end, the demographic section of the survey.

FIGURE 1. **Does your organization currently have recognition programs in place?**

	2005	2003	2002
Yes	89%	87%	84%
No	11%	13%	16%

Most Respondents Have Recognition Programs

An overwhelming majority (89 percent) of survey respondents have recognition programs in place in their organizations. This compares to 87 percent of respondents in the 2003 survey and 84 percent in the 2002 survey.

Most Respondents Have Not Eliminated Any Recognition Programs in Past 12 Months

Most organizations (89 percent) reported that they have not eliminated any recognition programs in the past year. Only about one in 10 respondents said their organization eliminated one or more recognition program(s) in the past

FIGURE 2. **Have you eliminated any recognition programs in the past 12 months?**

Yes	11%
No	89%

12 months. In the 2002 survey, an identical 89 percent of respondents who reported having a recognition program said they had not eliminated any programs during the previous 12 months.

About Half Are Looking at Starting New Recognition Programs in Next 12 Months

Almost half of respondents indicated that their organization is considering or planning to add new or expanded recognition programs in the next 12 months. In the 2003 survey, only about 40 percent of organizations reported that they were considering adding new or additional recognition programs in the near future.

FIGURE 3. **Are you considering implementing any new or additional recognition programs in the next 12 months?**

Yes	48%
No	52%

Ninety Percent Believe the Same or More Recognition Is Occurring Today vs. 12 Months Ago
Survey respondents' perception of the number of employee recognition incidents occurring within their organization seems mostly stable, with a combined 92 percent of respondents saying that there is about the same (52 percent) or more (40 percent) recognition occurring today versus 12 months ago in their organization.[1]

FIGURE 4. **Is there more or less recognition occurring (either formally or informally) in your organization today versus 12 months ago?**

<12 mo.	40%
>12 mo.	8%
=12 mo.	52%

Section II. Strategy, Goals and Measures of Recognition

After the first four questions, only those with employee recognition programs continued through the body of the survey. Those without recognition programs were asked to skip to the end, complete the demographic section and submit.

Sixty Percent Have a Written Recognition Strategy
Sixty percent of organizations have a written strategy regarding their employee recognition program(s), and 95 percent of those companies believe that it aligns with the overall organizational strategy. However, about two in five respondents (40 percent) report no written strategy behind their organization's recognition programs.

---

[1] *Although this is similar to a question asked previously, it has been made more specific and thus, comparison to previous surveys is not possible.*

FIGURE 5.

FIGURE 5. **Is there a written strategy behind your organization's recognition programs?** (Why they were created, the goals, etc.)

Yes	60%
No	40%

FIGURE 6. **Does your recognition strategy align with your organization's strategy?**

Yes	95%
No	5%

The No. 1 Goal of Recognition Programs (Again): Create a Positive Work Environment

When asked to select all of the goals of their organization's recognition programs, the top three answers for all three surveys (2002, 2003 and 2005) have been creating a positive work environment, motivating high performance and reinforcing desired behavior. In 2005, a newly added response, creating a culture of recognition, was the fourth most common goal selected by respondents.

Respondents that selected "other" in 2005 included comments such as: "to recognize years of service"' "to support becoming or remaining an employer of choice" and "to provide line of sight to company goals for employees." Responses in both 2003 and 2002 were very similar, with only a few exceptions slightly outside of the margin of error of the 2005 survey (+/-4%).

FIGURE 7. **What are the objectives/goals of your organization's recognition program?** (Check all that apply)

	2005	2003	2002
Create a positive work environment	81%	80%	84%
Motivate high performance	75%	75%	73%
Reinforce desired behavior	71%	75%	76%
Create a culture of recognition	70%	n/a	n/a
Increase morale	65%	71%	69%
Support organizational mission/values	62%	66%	68%
Increase retention or decrease turnover	49%	51%	51%
Encourage loyalty	38%	40%	45%
Support a culture change	23%	24%	23%
Other (please specify)	3%	5%	9%

Three in Four Believe Recognition Programs are Meeting Goals
More than three-fourths (76 percent) of respondents feel that the recognition
programs are meeting their established objectives and goals. In the 2002
survey, a similar 78 percent answered in the affirmative. Only 24 percent in
2005 believe that their programs are not meeting goals.

FIGURE 8. **Do you feel your programs are meeting the objectives/goals?**

Yes	76%
No	24%

Employee Satisfaction Survey is Top Success Measure for Recognition Programs
More than a third of respondents (36 percent) in 2005 said their organization
does not measure the success of their recognition programs. For those that are
measuring success, employee satisfaction surveys are used most commonly,
with about 45 percent of companies using this gauge. Usage and/or participation rates and the number of nominations made to recognition program(s)
also are commonly used indicators of the success by companies in 2005.

FIGURE 9. **What measurements for success do you use in your recognition programs?**
(Check all that apply)

	2005
Employee satisfaction surveys	45%
Usage and/or participation rates	32%
Number of nominations	31%
Turnover	20%
Customer surveys	15%
Productivity	15%
Return on investment (ROI)	9%
We do not measure success of the program(s)	36%

Section III. Structure and Types of Recognition Programs

Most Organizations Have Both Formal and Informal Recognition Programs
Most respondents (71 percent) indicated in 2005 that their organization offers
both formal and informal recognition programs — similar to percentages in
the previous two surveys. In the survey, formal programs are defined as
planned recognition programs (e.g., attendance, performance, safety, years of

service, etc.), while informal programs are spontaneous gestures of appreciation (nonmonetary or of small monetary value).

FIGURE 10. **What types of recognition programs are included in your recognition strategy?**

	2005	2003	2002
Formal Only	19%	16%	17%
Informal Only	9%	9%	10%
Both	71%	72%	70%
Other	1%	3%	3%

*Most Organizations Have Both Organizationwide and Department-Specific
Recognition Programs*
Just over half (52 percent) of respondents reported recognition programs that
are both organizationwide and department-specific, while 38 percent indicated that their recognition programs are companywide only. Just 7 percent stated that their recognition programs are department-specific. A handful of
respondents selected other and indicated that their programs vary greatly
among different subsidiaries or by type of employee. Data from the 2003
survey is nearly identical to Figure 11, with 43 percent saying "companywide,"
5 percent reporting "department specific" 49 percent "both" and a 3-percent
"other" response.

FIGURE 11. **Are your recognition programs ...**

Companywide	38%
Department-specific	7%
Both	52%
Other	3%

*'Length of Service' Is the Most Common Recognition Program; 'Above
and Beyond' Is Second*
As in both 2002 and 2003, the most prevalent type of recognition program
offered by organizations in 2005 is for length of service. Of the 89 percent
that offer this program today, 87 percent have offered it for at least five years
— so this program is very common and established. Most of the recognition
programs listed in Figure 11 were reported by respondents to have been
offered for longer than one year and, for many programs, respondents say
their organization has been offering them for more than five years. For example,

of the 51 percent of organizations that have an established retirement recognition program, 91 percent have been offering the program for more than five years. Similar frequencies were revealed in the previous two surveys.

Respondents whose companies offer other various programs were asked to share the types of programs. Below are both the most common among the "other" responses and some of the most unique and innovative programs mentioned:

- Major family event (birth, adoption, marriage, etc.)
- Thank You
- President's award
- Programs to motivate specific behaviors (customer service, production, etc.)
- Patent or invention
- Peer-to-peer or employee-to-employee
- Cost reduction or savings
- Educational achievement

FIGURE 12. **What types of formal recognition programs do you offer, and how long have they been in place?**

Length of service	89%
Above and beyond performance	87%
Sales performance	51%
Retirement	51%
Suggestions/Ideas	41%
Employee of the year, month, etc.	36%
Safety performance	33%
Attendance	22%
Other, if applicable (please specify)	10%

If offered, for how long?

	>5 yrs	1-5 yrs	>12 mo.
Retirement	91%	8%	1%
Length of service	87%	11%	2%
Sales performance	70%	22%	8%
Attendance	66%	30%	4%
Employee of the year, month, etc.	57%	33%	10%
Safety performance	53%	35%	12%
Suggestion/ideas	46%	42%	12%
Above and beyond performance	46%	43%	11%
Other, if applicable (please specify)	46%	38%	16%

'Length of Service' Is Most Frequently Awarded Recognition
Consistent with their status as the most commonly offered recognition programs in 2005, "length of service" and "above and beyond performance" also recorded the highest percentage of employees who were recognized during the past 12 months. The number of employees recognized under each of the programs is related to the type of plan and subsequent employee eligibility, but the responses in Figure 13 indicate under which programs the most employee recognition is occurring. Respondents in the "other" category revealed the same types of programs reflected in Figure 12.

FIGURE 13. **For the programs your organization offers, what percentage of your employees were recognized in the past 12 months within each program?**

	2005	2003	2002
Length of service	25%	28%	29%
Above and beyond performance	19%	21%	21%
Safety performance	16%	21%	24%
Attendance	16%	26%	19%
Sales performance	14%	22%	13%
Retirement	11%	n/a	n/a
Suggestion/ideas	7%	11%	10%
Employee of the year, month, etc.	6%	10%	6%
Other (please specify)	18%	n/a	22%

Special Events, One-On-One with Manager and Staff Meetings Are Most Common Recognition Venues
It is not surprising that companies are using a variety of different methods to present recognition awards. Depending on the type of recognition or award, most companies are recognizing employees at special events (70 percent), one-on-one meetings with managers (67 percent) and in staff meetings (60 percent). Another 36 percent said their organization also presents recognition awards in companywide meetings. Among the "other" answers: intranet announcements, newsletter articles and presentations during trainings or board meetings.

FIGURE 14. **Where are recognition awards presented? (Check all that apply.)**

	2005	2003	2002
Special event	70%	63%	65%
One-on-one with manager	67%	69%	63%
Staff meeting	60%	59%	59%
Companywide meeting	36%	37%	33%
Not presented	10%	7%	n/a
Other (please specify)	3%	10%	11%

Certificates/Plaques and Cash Are Still Top Recognition Items

Organizations are using a variety of tangible items to recognize employees. (See Figure 15.) The most common tangible awards are certificates and plaques, followed by cash, company logo merchandise and gift certificates. The dispersion of responses in Figure 15 demonstrates that companies are offering multiple or different awards for different programs. This variety of award types gives employees an opportunity to earn rewards that meet their wants and needs, which, in turn, increases the motivation to meet the goals of any given recognition program. Respondents also were able to provide examples of "other" types of items that are being presented as recognition awards:

- Food (breakfast, lunch, steak/crab feeds, pizza parties, etc.)
- Stock
- Paid time off/holidays
- Employee drawings.

FIGURE 15. **What types of items are presented as recognition awards? (Check all that apply.)**

	2005	2003	2002
Certificates and/or plaques	81%	75%	n/a
Cash	58%	63%	58%
Company logo merchandise	57%	51%	n/a
Gift certificates for products/items	57%	57%	63%
Jewelry	44%	43%	40%
Office accessories	38%	41%	41%
Household items	38%	34%	35%
Recreational items/sporting goods	29%	n/a	n/a
Electronics	28%	24%	24%
Gift certificates for personal services	25%	26%	n/a
Travel	21%	17%	14%
Timepieces	21%	33%	28%
Other (please specify)	8%	23%	31%

Section IV. Program Administration and Support

In Most Organizations, HR Administers Recognition Programs
More than half of all respondents (57 percent) said that the human resources department is primarily responsible for administering recognition programs. Among the remaining 43 percent of respondents, 15 percent said that each department in the organization is responsible for its own recognition program administration and another 11 percent reported that the compensation department has responsibility for all recognition programs. Most of the 8 percent that selected "other" revealed that recognition program administration is handled through cross-functional teams.

FIGURE 16. **What department is responsible for administering the majority of your organization's recognition programs?**

	2005	2003
Human resources	57%	48%
Each department in the organization is responsible for own program administration	15%	15%
Compensation	11%	12%
Benefits	3%	3%
Organizational development	3%	n/a
Corporate communications	2%	3%
Training	1%	n/a
Other (please specify)	8%	19%

Most Organizations Do Not have a Full-Time Position Dedicated to Recognition
While human resource departments most commonly have administrative responsibility for recognition programs, the vast majority of organizations do not have a full-time, dedicated position responsible for recognition administration. The 16 percent that do have a full-time position indicated having an average of 2.6 full-time equivalent (FTE) employees dedicated to recognition. Twenty-six percent of respondents indicated that their organization dedicates portions of employee time — on average, about 20 percent of the week is spent on recognition programs. There were a handful of respondents who selected "other" and indicated that the position responsible for program administration varies by program and/or type of employees.

FIGURE 17. **What position is responsible for administering the recognition program(s)?**

Full-time dedicated position(s)	16%
Position within department above dedicated part time	26%
No one position is responsible for the program, it is a shared responsibility among the department personnel	52%
Other (please specify)	6%

Respondents were asked to identify the job title(s) of the position(s) primarily responsible for recognition program administration. There were a variety of responses, however most could be categorized within one of the following groups and tended to have human resources or compensation and benefits in the title:

- VP of human resources, total rewards or compensation and benefits
- Senior level within HR, compensation and/or benefits but not VP
- Manager (operational or corporate/administrative)
- Recognition coordinator
- Analyst (typically compensation or benefits analyst)

Most Organizations Have a Specific Budget for Recognition Programs

Sixty-nine percent of respondents indicated that their organization has a specific budget for recognition programs. Among this group, the average respondent sets aside roughly 3.8 percent of payroll budget for recognition programs.

When respondents who indicated their organization has a specific recognition budget were asked whether the budget is centralized (entire organization), specific to each department budget or a combination of both, significant dispersion was revealed. Forty percent said their budget is for the entire organization, 37 percent said it was both centralized and department specific, and about 23 percent said it is up to departments.

FIGURE 18. **Is there a budget for your recognition programs?**

	2005	2003	2002
Yes	69%	71%	62%
No	31%	29%	38%

FIGURE 19. **Is the recognition budget:**

Centralized for the entire organization	40%
Held in each specific departmental budget	23%
Centralized or department-specific	37%

Most Believe Management Shows Better Than Moderate Support for Recognition
Respondents were asked to provide an opinion about the degree to which
their organization's senior management team supports recognition programs
(1-7 scale with 1 defined as showing "no support at all" and 7 as showing a
"high level of support"). The vast majority (84 percent) believes management
shows "moderate" support or better, with almost half of all respondents giving either a 6 or 7 rating. The overall average rating (mean) rating among all
respondents was 5.1.

FIGURE 20. **What level of support do you feel your organization's senior management team shows
for your recognition programs?**

7 (High level of support)	19%
6	30%
5	19%
4 (Moderate support)	17%
3	10%
2	5%
1 (No support at all)	1%

Most Believe Management Views Recognition as an Investment, Not an Expense
Consistent with the results in Figure 21, the majority of respondents (55 percent) believe senior management views recognition programs as an investment,
not an expense. Slightly less than a third of respondents are unsure of senior
management's viewpoint on recognition programs, perhaps an indication that
staff working on recognition need to do a better job of communicating and
proactively providing positive information to senior management.

FIGURE 21. **Which of the following best describes how senior management in your organization views employee recognition programs?**

As an investment	55%
As an expense	13%
Unsure	32%

Wide Disparity of Practices for Recognition of International Employees
Among the 38 percent of respondents whose organizations have employees outside of North America, 92 percent say that their international employees participate in recognition programs that are either North America-based or foreign-based. The largest percentage of respondents (34 percent) said their programs allow international employees to participate in the same recognition programs as North America-based employees. Another 30 percent have recognition programs that are exclusive to international employees and not based on North America.

FIGURE 22. **(If your organization has employees outside of N. America ...) Which of the following best describes the recognition programs for those employees?**

International employees participate in all or most of the same recognition programs as North America-based employees	34%
International employees participate in a few of the same recognition programs as North America-based employees	10%
International employees participate in some of their own programs and some of the same recognition programs as North America-based employees	18%
International employees have their own recognition programs	30%
International employees do not currently participate in any recognition programs	8%

Section V. Recognition Program Communication and Training

Company Newsletter and Employee Orientation Are Most Common Communication Tools
Companies use a variety of methods to communicate and promote recognition programs to employees. The organizational newsletter is the most common method (53 percent), with employee orientation (46 percent) and posters, flyers, etc. (34 percent) also being prominent vehicles for communication. Another 10 percent selected "other" and indicated that their organization communicates recognition programs in staff meetings, special events (luncheons,

etc.) and department-specific newsletters. Although it may be difficult to believe, one in 10 (10%) indicated that the company does not have a communication plan for recognition programs.

FIGURE 23. **What media do you use to communicate your recognition programs? (Check all that apply.)**

Company newsletter	53%
Employee orientation	46%
Posters, flyers and/or table tents	36%
Employee handbook	30%
Other (please specify)	10%
We do not have a communications plan	10%

Few Have a Formal Training Program for Recognition; And Most Often it is In-Person Training

While the majority of organizations have communication plans for their recognition programs, formal training programs for managers are much less common. Only 23 percent of respondents reported that a formal training program for recognition programs exists within their companies. The organizations that are committed to formal training programs for managers typically rely on in-person training sessions (69 percent). Other formal training is delivered through online education, and handbooks are used by more than a third of respondents' organizations. For respondents' organizations using "other" methods, common responses included training in management meetings, through e-mail and/or added to group training on other topics.

FIGURE 24. **Do you have a formal training program for managers about your recognition programs?**

Yes	23%
No	77%

FIGURE 25. **If yes, what formal training methods do you use to train your managers? (Check all that apply.)**

In-person training session	69%
Online education	36%
Handbook	36%
Video	8%
Other (please specify)	17%

Most Organizations Use Intranet or Internet for Program Communication
More than ever, organizations are relying more on electronic media and technology to communicate and administer many of their total rewards programs. Indeed, this is also true with recognition programs. More than half of all respondents (54 percent) indicated using electronic means to communicate recognition programs, and a strong 43 percent have come to rely on the ease of online award-ordering systems that allow employees to choose their reward and minimize administration efforts. Internet and intranet capabilities also allow nomination processes, general administration, and reporting and tracking of awards to be handled with ease; more than a third are using electronic media to administer these components.

FIGURE 26. **Do any of your recognition programs utilize electronic media or communications (e.g., Internet/intranet) for any of the following? (Check all that apply.)**

	2005	2003	2002
Program communication	54%	40%	72%
Award ordering	43%	35%	61%
Award nomination	42%	29%	49%
Program administration	36%	24%	38%
Program reporting and/or tracking	33%	19%	32%
Program training	12%	10%	n/a
None of our programs utilize the Internet/intranet	27%	n/a	53%

Respondent Demographics

Number of Employees:

Less than 100	13%
100 - 499	15%
500 - 999	6%
1,000 - 2,499	17%
2,500 - 4,999	16%
5,000 - 9,999	12%
10,000 - 19,999	6%
20,000 or more	16%

Industry:

Services	35%
Manufacturing	24%
Finance and Insurance	18%
Transportation and Utility	7%
Public Administration	6%
Retail	4%
Wholesale	2%
Other	5%

Affiliation:

WorldatWork member	35%
NAER member	24%
Both	18%

Responsibility Level:

Senior Executive/Director/Vice President	33%
Manager/Assistant Director	33%
Senior Analyst/Analyst	22%
Supervisor	5%
Consultant	5%
Educator	0%
Other	2%

2003 Recognition Survey

A Joint Survey by WorldatWork and NAER

Recognition is an important component of an organization's total rewards program and is instrumental in reducing turnover, increasing productivity and creating a positive work environment. When employees realize their contributions are important to a company's success, they are more likely to embrace the organization's mission, goals and values.

A September 2003 survey, conducted by WorldatWork and the National Association for Employee Recognition (NAER), shows that employee recognition continues to be important to organizations, and they are making it an integral part of their mission and people strategy. They also are thinking more strategically about the different rewards offered for different types of programs, and which rewards are most valuable to employees.

Methodology

For the third year in a row, WorldatWork and NAER surveyed a sample of members to understand what companies are doing with recognition programs. Surveys were sent electronically to a random representative sample of 2,748 WorldatWork members and to all 520 NAER members. A total of 413 responses were received — a 13 percent response rate.

The survey responses can be considered statistically representative of the WorldatWork membership. The typical WorldatWork member is at or above the manager level in compensation, benefits or human resources, working in the headquarters of a large company in North America. Ninety-five percent of the *Fortune* 1,000 companies have at least one employee who is a WorldatWork member.

Summary of Key Findings
- Recognition continues to be important to organizations, with 87 percent of companies using recognition programs as part of their people strategy.
- Forty percent of companies are doing more with recognition than 12 months ago, while only 12 percent are doing less than 12 months ago.
- Of those companies with a recognition program, 65 percent have a written strategy and 97 percent of those feel it aligns with their organizational strategy and links directly to what matters most to the organization.

- Two-thirds of companies measure the success of their recognition programs. The most common metrics are employee satisfaction surveys (67 percent) and the number of nominations (50 percent).
- There is a companywide recognition budget in 43% of organizations, compared to 38 percent where the budget is department specific.
- The majority of companies (87 percent) use length of service as the foundation for their recognition program. Companies also are adding other program types, including "above and beyond performance" (85 percent), sales (43 percent), suggestions (36 percent), employee of the period (29 percent), safety (28 percent) and attendance (20 percent).
- Human resources administers the majority (48 percent) of recognition programs.
- The Internet has facilitated the immediacy of recognition programs, as more companies are using technology to enhance their programs.
- Companies are providing a wide range of recognition awards that are meaningful to employees (plaques, gift certificates, jewelry, household items, travel, etc.).
- Only 20 percent of companies have a formal training program to educate managers about recognition programs, and 75 percent of these companies use an in-person training session.
- Recognition programs need to be used and communicated frequently to let employees know they exist.

Detailed Findings

Of the 413 respondents, 87 percent currently have a recognition program in place. This figure is similar to 2002, when the survey found 84 percent of 391 respondents had a recognition program.

FIGURE 1. **Does your organization currently have recognition programs in place?**

Yes	87%
No	13%

Additionally, many organizations have expanded their recognition programs in the past year, with 40 percent of respondents indicating they are doing more with their recognition programs than 12 months ago.

More	40%
About the Same	48%
Less	12%

Of responding companies who do not currently have recognition programs in place, 37 percent are considering implementing new programs in the next 12 months. Forty percent of companies with programs already in place are considering implementing additional programs in the next 12 months.

FIGURE 3. **Are you considering implementing any new or additional programs in the next 12 months?**

	Currently Have Programs	Do No Have Programs
Yes	40%	37%
No	60%	63%

Recognition Strategy and Goals

Sixty-five percent of respondents have a written strategy behind their recognition programs and, of those, 97 percent feel that the strategy aligns with their overall organizational strategy.

Creating a positive work environment is the most prevalent goal of a recognition program, chosen by 80 percent of respondents. A close second and third were creating a culture of recognition (76 percent) and motivating high performance (75 percent).

FIGURE 4. **What are the objectives/goals of your organization's recognition programs? (Check all that apply.)**

Create a positive work environment	80%
Create a culture of recognition	76%
Motivate high performance	75%
Reinforce desired behaviors	75%
Increase morale	71%
Support organizational mission/values	66%
Increase retention/decrease turnover	51%
Encourage loyalty	40%
Support a culture change	24%
Other	5%

Eight in 10 respondents believe their recognition programs are meeting the program's goals and objectives. For two-thirds of respondents, this belief is supported by an actual measurement of success. The most commonly used metrics for recognition programs are employee satisfaction surveys (67 percent) and the number of nominations (50 percent).

FIGURE 5. **What measurements for success do you use in your recognition programs? (Check all that apply.)**

Employee satisfaction surveys	67%
Number of nominations	50%
Turnover	28%
Productivity	25%
Customer surveys	22%
Usage rates/participation rates	21%
ROI (return on investment)	15%

Types of Recognition Programs

Most responding organizations offer both formal and informal recognition programs. As defined by the survey, formal programs are structured or planned recognition programs (e.g., attendance, performance, safety, years of service, etc.), while informal programs are spontaneous gestures of appreciation (nonmonetary or of small monetary value).

FIGURE 6. **What types of recognition programs are included in your recognition strategy?**

Formal	16%
Informal	9%
Combination of Both	72%
Other	3%

Respondents offer recognition programs both companywide and as department-specific.

FIGURE 7. **Are your recognition programs:**

Companywide	43%
Department-specific	5%
Both	49%
Other	3%

Eighty-seven percent of respondents use length-of-service awards, and 85 percent of responding organizations use performance ("above and beyond") awards. Less commonly used programs are attendance (used by 20 percent) and safety awards (28 percent).

FIGURE 8. **Types of formal programs offered:**

Length of service	87%
Performance/Above & Beyond	85%
Sales	43%
Suggestions	36%
Employee of the period	29%
Safety	28%
Attendance	20%

Length-of-service awards also have been in place for the longest period of time in most companies, with 87 percent of respondents indicating they have had this program in place for more than five years.

FIGURE 9. **Length of time programs have been in place**

	< 12 months	1–5 years	> 5 years
Length of service	3%	10%	87%
Sales	8%	30%	62%
Employee of the period	12%	30%	58%
Attendance	9%	37%	54%
Safety	8%	39%	53%
Performance/Above & Beyond	10%	45%	45%
Suggestions/Ideas	14%	42%	44%

Responding organizations award length-of-service awards to the most employees annually. On average, companies report awarding 28 percent of the employee population a length-of-service award in the past 12 months. In contrast, companies, on average, report 10 percent of the employee population receives an "employee-of-the-period" award annually.

FIGURE 10. **Percentage of Employees Recognized in the Past 12 Months**

Length of service	28%
Attendance	26%
Sales	22%
Performance/Above & Beyond	21%
Safety	21%
Suggestions	11%
Employee of the period	10%

Program Administration

Almost half of organizations (48 percent) administer their recognition programs through HR.

FIGURE 11. **What department is responsible for administering the majority of your organization's recognition program(s)?**

Human Resources	48%
Each department is responsible for its own program	15%
Compensation	12%
Corporate Communications	3%
Benefits	3%
Other	19%

"Other" mentions in Figure 11 include work-life, marketing, administration or a combination of HR and another department. Only 14 percent of respondents have a full-time position dedicated to recognition programs. Thirty-six percent of respondents have a part-time position within a department dedicated to recognition programs. On average, this person spends about 10 percent of the workweek on recognition programs. The vast majority of respondents (42 percent) indicated that no one position is responsible for the program; it is a shared responsibility among the department personnel. Another 8 percent of respondents have other types of shared responsibilities for administering the program, mainly a committee or a recognition team.

FIGURE 12. **What position is responsible for administering the recognition program(s)?**

Full-time dedicated position(s)	14%
Position within department dedicated part-time	36%
No one position is responsible for the program	42%
Other	8%

Seven in 10 responding organizations have a budget for their recognition programs.

FIGURE 13. **Is there a dedicated budget for your recognition programs?**

Yes	71%
No	29%

FIGURE 14. **Is the recognition budget:**

Centralized for the entire organization	62%
Held in each specific departmental budget	38%

On average, responding organizations indicate that their recognition program budget is 2.0 percent of payroll, with a median of 1.0 percent.

Communication, Training, and Award Presentation and Types

Nearly nine in 10 (87 percent) of organizations with recognition programs have a communications plan for their program. (See Figure 1.) The Intranet is the most widely used communication vehicle (66 percent), followed by company newsletters and employee orientation (50 percent). Other vehicles used are: company e-mail, fliers and posters.

FIGURE 15. **What media do you use to communicate your recognition programs? (Check all that apply.)**

Intranet/Internet	66%
Company newsletter	50%
Employee orientation	50%
Employee handbook	29%
Other	21%

Only 20 percent of organizations have a formal training program for managers about the recognition programs. The most commonly used training method is an in-person session.

FIGURE 16. **What formal training methods do you use to train your managers? (Check all that apply.)**

In-person training session	75%
Handbook	36%
Online education	21%
Other	12%
Video	10%

Managers present most awards one-on-one to the recipient (69 percent), while 63 percent of organizations hold a special event to recognize award presentations. Department meetings were the most cited "other" presentation method.

FIGURE 17. **How are recognition awards presented? (Check all that apply.)**

One-on-one with manager	69%
Special event (banquet, luncheon, etc.)	63%
Staff meeting	59%
Companywide meeting	37%
Other	10%
Not presented (mailed to home)	7%

FIGURE 18. **Do any of your recognition programs use the Internet for any of the following? (Check all that apply.)**

Program communication	40%
Award ordering	35%
Award nomination	29%
Program administration	24%
Program reporting/tracking	19%
Training	10%

Certificates and plaques are the most popular awards, awarded by 75 percent of respondents. Second is cash, awarded by 63 percent and third are product gift certificates, awarded by 57percent.

FIGURE 19. **What types of items are presented as recognition awards? (Check all that apply.)**

Certificates/Plaques	75%
Cash	63%
Gift certificates for products/item purchases	57%
Company logo merchandise	51%
Jewelry (e.g. necklaces, lapel pins, bracelets, etc.)	43%
Office accessories (e.g. desk sets, portfolios, pen/pencil sets, etc.)	41%
Household items (e.g. crystal vases, china, etc.)	34%
Watches	33%
Gift certifications for personal services (e.g. spa treatments, car washes, etc.)	26%
Electronics (e.g. cameras, TVs, stereos, etc.)	24%
Other	23%
Travel	17%

Respondent Demographics

Company Size:

Less than 100	10%
100 - 499	13%
500 - 999	8%
1,000 - 2,499	15%
2,500 - 4,999	13%
5,000 - 9,999	13%
10,000 or more	28%

Industry:

Manufacturing	23%
Finance & Insurance	16%
Health care & Social Assistance	9%
Professional, Scientific & Technical Services	8%
Information	5%
Utilities	5%
Public Administration	5%
Other Services (except Public Administration)	5%
Retail Trade	3%
Educational Services	3%
Accommodations & Food Services	2%
Transportation & Warehousing	2%
Real Estate & Rental & Leasing	2%
Arts, Entertainment & Recreation	2%
Wholesale Trade	1%
Other	8%

RECOGNITION LOG			
EMPLOYEE NAME	DESCRIPTION OF ACTION, PERFORMANCE OR EVENT	WHO OBSERVED ACTION OR EVENT?	WHAT MAKES PERFORMANCE OR ACTION EXCEPTIONAL?

WHAT STANDARDS WERE USED?	WHEN DID THE ACTION OR EVENT OCCUR?	WHAT TYPE OF RECOGNITION WAS GIVEN TO THE EMPLOYEE?	

Selected References

WorldatWork Articles

Abrahamsen, Lane. 2003. Employers Turn to Recognition to Motivate Employees. *workspan*, December, 24-26.

Armitage, Amelia. 2004. Overcoming the 'Elephant Problem': Creating Value with Corporate Performance Management through Strategic Alignment and Engagement. *WorldatWork Journal*, Third Quarter, 34-45.

Batutis, Susan. 2002. Money Talks for Northeastern University Employees. *workspan*, August, 44-47.

Blackburn, Jan; Bremen, John M. 2003. From Exporting to Integrating: Optimizing Total Rewards for a Global Sales Force. *WorldatWork Journal*, Fourth Quarter, 72-79.

Cilmi, Amy Parr. 2005. Managers: The Critical Link in a Successful Rewards and Recognition Program. *workspan*, November, 19-22.

Dermer, Michael. 2005. Ovation: NBC Universal's Recognition Program Sparks Employee Engagement. *workspan*, May, 39-42.

Dobbs, Kevin. 2005. On-Demand Rewards and Recognition Programs: The Right Vendor Equals Success. *workspan*, November, 24-26.

Gostick, Adrian. 2003. A Hero's Welcome: Improving Culture with Noncash Awards and Recognition, *workspan*, July, 44-47.

Gostick, Adrian. 2000. They Do Recognition Right. *workspan*, October, 34-36.

Green, Gordon T. 2005. Recognition and the Generational Divide. *workspan*, November, 10-11.

Handel, Jeremy. 2001. Recognition: Pats on the Back Motivate Employees. *workspan*, December, 36-38.

Kasiarz, David; Purushotham, Daniel. 2004. Recognition Ruse. Focus on Ethics, *workspan*, May, 104.

Keegan, Brendan P. 2002. Incentive Programs Boost Employee Morale and Productivity. *workspan*, March, 30-33.

Kelley, Pat. 2002. Revisiting Maslow: Motivation, Retention and Performance after Sept. 11. *workspan*, May, 50-56.

McKibbin-Brown, Lynn. 2003. Beyond the Gold Watch: Employee Recognition Today. *workspan*, April, 44-46.

Parus, Barbara. 2004. Recognizing and Retaining Worker "Bs". *workspan*, March, 46-48.

Parus, Barbara. 2002. Recognition: A Strategic Tool for Retaining Talent. *workspan*, November, 14-18.

Satterfield, Terry. 2003. From Performance Management to Performance Leadership: A Model for Change. *WorldatWork Journal*, First Quarter, 15-20.

Serino, Bonnie. 2002. Noncash Awards Boost Sales Compensation Plans. *workspan*, August, 24-27.

Taylor, Tom. 2004. Dispelling the Myths about Peer Recognition Programs. *workspan*, December, 47-49.

Young, Marjorie; Roach, John. 2003. Accentuate the Positives. *workspan*, May, 50-52.

WorldatWork Surveys (www.worldatwork.org/library/research&surveys)

2005 Trends in Employee Recognition

2002 Employee Recognition Survey

WorldatWork Courses (www.worldatwork.org/education/compensation)

C12: Variable Pay: Incentives, Recognition and Bonuses

GR6: Variable Pay: Incentives, Recognition and Bonuses

T1: Total Rewards Management

WorldatWork Publications (www.worldatwork.org/bookstore)

Hay, Donald. 2004. *Maximizing the Impact of Recognition*. Scottsdale: WorldatWork.

2001. Life at Work – *Beyond Compensation and Benefits*. Scottsdale: WorldatWork.

Other Publications (www.worldatwork.org/bookstore)

Gostick, Adrian; Elton, Chester. 2004. *A Carrot A Day – A Daily Dose of Recognition For Your Employees.* Layton: Gibbs Smith.

Gostick, Adrian; Elton, Chester. 2002. *The 24-Carrot Manager Recognition Toolkit.* Layton: Gibbs Smith.

Gostick, Adrian; Elton, Chester. 2001. *Managing With Carrots.* Layton: Gibbs Smith.

Manas, Todd M.; Graham, Michael Dennis. 2003. *Creating a Total Rewards Strategy – A Toolkit for Designing Business-Based Plans.* New York, AMACOM.

Nelson, Bob; Spitzer, Dean. 2003. *The 1001 Rewards & Recognition Fieldbook The Complete Guide.* New York: Workman Publishing.

Ventrice, Cindy. 2003. *Make Their Day! Employee Recognition That Works!* San Francisco: Berrett-Koehler.

Wilson, Thomas B. 2003. *Innovative Reward Systems for the Changing Workplace.* New York: McGraw Hill.